Edgar Fawcett

Song and story, later poems

Edgar Fawcett

Song and story, later poems

ISBN/EAN: 9783743328440

Manufactured in Europe, USA, Canada, Australia, Japa

Cover: Foto ©ninafisch / pixelio.de

Manufactured and distributed by brebook publishing software (www.brebook.com)

Edgar Fawcett

Song and story, later poems

CONTENTS.

	PAGE
ALAN ELIOT	7
THE REPUBLIC	51
THE SINGING OF LUIGI	66
THE RIVERS	74
A VENGEANCE	92
A MOOD OF CLEOPATRA	96
THE GIRL AT THE CROSSING	104
IDEALS	107
THE DOUBTER	112
CYNICISM	120
PORTENT	123
YESTERDAY	125
NATURE IN BONDAGE	129
MYSTERIES	131
SELF-DENIAL	133
THE POET'S MASQUE	135
A LEGEND OF HARVEST	139
A WHITE CAMELLIA	142
ROCKS	144
THE OLD GARDEN	146
A GERMAN CRADLE-SONG	149
CRICKET-CRIES	151

CONTENTS.

	PAGE
WOUNDS	155
REMEMBERED LOVE	159
THE PUNISHMENT	160
AN OLD BEAU	161
CONSOLATION	162
ENVY	163
MEISSONIER	164

SONNETS.

BETROTHAL	167
CROWNS	168
SATIETY	169
THE HOURS	170
INTERREGNUM	171
THE DIAMOND	172
AMOUR TERRESTRE	173
INDIAN SUMMER	174
BEES	175
A TIGER-LILY	176
SLEEP'S THRESHOLD	177
THE SPHINX OF ICE	178
ON THE NEWPORT CLIFFS	179
TO MAURICE THOMPSON	180
TO OSCAR WILDE	181

SONG AND STORY.

ALAN ELIOT.

THE old house where Alan Eliot first saw light
   Was hidden among dark intermingling pines,
A meadowy ramble from that savage coast
Against whose myriad-harbored ruggedness
The Atlantic, as if ired that Maine should be,
Tumbles his cold tempestuous emerald. Here
The spacious homestead rose, to its neighbor sea,
Through prim dull rooms and silent shadowed halls,
Grown murmurously kinned, like an upflung shell.

Child voices, in past years, had gayly rung
Out among these lone paths where now the weed
Pushed rank disfeaturing leafage; in the dusk
Of these now desolate chambers brilliant smiles
From blooming mouths had burst; these wordless walls

Where grim occasional Eliots posed in paint,
Had heard the adoring vows of lover-lips
That now were dust; and higher, in attic rooms,
Great odorous chests held fragments of the past,
Spicily buried there by buried hands, —
The grandam's ancient neckerchief beside
The babe's robe and the yellowing bridal veil.

And yet the old homestead was not masterless,
For Alan Eliot dwelt here, loving well
The slow consecutive quietudes of days,
Linked like calm pools; and blithely, now and then,
Like a sudden bright-clad butterfly in a wood,
His brother Adrian, fresh from college bonds,
Would speed, with shining eyes of larkspur-blue
And sunny locks and rich mellifluous laugh,
To the still shade of Alan's library,
Deep under spells of tome and globe and bust.

"Bat of the unwholesome book-shelf," he would cry,
"Profit by nature's courteous accident
That made you brother to the auroral lark!
Come, blink and flutter awhile in open sun!"
And Alan — for he had loved with utter love
This boy, a decade younger than himself,
Since first his name left Adrian's lisping lips —

Would rise, and throwing down whate'er he read,
Walk seaward o'er the lawns at Adrian's side,
Heeding the lad's felicitous fluencies,
Watching him paint, with quick yet forceful brush,
On canvas of collegiate anecdote,
Pictures where many a sacred rule defied,
And many a foolish escapade, stood out
From backgrounds dark with professorial wrath.

And now when Adrian, having overswept
The full curriculum into seniorhood,
Came home with a small modest honor, won
Lightly, and worn yet lightlier, like a rose,
To Alan, as near the shore they strolled, he spoke
(While the deep blue of heaven, one summer morn,
Looked all its soul out into the bland sea),
With words whose hardy vehemence might have stung
But for the watchful love that instantly
Healed what it hurt; and Adrian's words were these:

"O Alan, it is not well with you, not well!
You have made the mind the body's sepulchre;
You have thwarted manhood's genial equipoise;
The alert red blood, that feeds on light and air,
You have thinned amid the darkness and the damp
Of those long murky vaults that history's hand

Paves with the whitening bones of dead men's thought.
Ah, brother, this grave paleness on your cheek
Meets dissonantly morning's radiant cheer,
And all this amethyst amplitude of sea
Can glass no flash of joy in your dulled eyes!
Look you, I pluck one delicate dandelion;
Touch to your nostril its cool feathery gold,
And tell me, does the aroma, faint and fresh
As though, days off, the ambrosial rosy foot
Of Hebe had softly touched it, thrilling it,
Bear to you no consolatory balm,
No chaste intangible spell that never hid
In all proud Alexandria's ruined scrolls?
But, Alan, if you are mindful of my love,
My brother-love that fondly looks to you
As sire and brother interblent in one,
Being like a vine too bounteous for its prop,
O'erflowing this with deeps of lavish leaves,—
O Alan, if you are mindful of such love,
Hereafter cloak yourself not all in gloom,
Forget your books for a little space each day,
Companion me in drive or walk or sail,
And let the alluring summer start your sap,
Till stubborn boughs with richer greenery
Welcome this love of mine that holds your love
As dearer boon than ever bough to bird!"

Then Adrian saw on Alan's firm lean face
A smile that wholly bathed it, as the sun
Bathes a dark sea-crag in aerial gold;
And flinging an arm about his brother's neck,
While leisurely they sauntered seaward thus
(A wan-browed scholar with thought-furrowed face,
A merry-eyed athlete, deft at oar and ball),
Adrian made happy plans for future hours.
And "We shall see, next winter," he gayly said,
"No splintry icicles hang brittle spears
Among the shivering pines, nor hear the howl
Of wolfish winds at the jarred homestead-panes,
Nor the wild riotous clash of wave on strand.
But we shall sail the blue Neapolitan bay,
Or breathe the empurpled Roman air, or watch
From gondolas the Venetian moonlight clothe
Pale immemorial sculptured palaces.
For though we are thus dissimilar, we two,
Still there is that in either's life which leans
Invisible arms toward those old storied lands.
Meanwhile 't were best if I could win you forth
A little among those neighbor village-folk,
Our parents' friends — and in departed years
Kindliest of friends to us, but now estranged
By dumb discourtesy of neglect, though chilled
To ice that one full smile would quickly thaw."

And Alan answered then, with positiveness,
"Rome, Naples, all sweet Italy, if you will,
But not that garrulous village, packed with spite,
A-buzz with scandalous bees, a gossip-hive."
Yet Adrian pleaded hard, and gained at length
A part if not the entirety of his will.
For Alan went with him, on a near day,
To visit one whom their dead sire had loved,
Old Lemuel Lane, once village-minister,
But sitting now, at seventy years and five,
Tired out beside the toilful road of life,
As laborers pause at evening ere they walk
Homeward to rest, and dreamily overhead
The twilight tinges heaven; so Lemuel sat,
Calm in the dying twilight of his life,
Its peaceful glimmerings on his silver hair,
And voices from the far past calling him,
Vague as the tremulous night-breeze in deep boughs.

He had been no gentle zealot, in his time,
For the rigid creed he clung to, Lemuel Lane.
From the prim altar of his plain-built church,
When the hardy biceps yet was in its prime,
He had pounded his good share of the " awful wrath
And scathing vengeance of eternal God."
Yet though he had preached for half a century

Apocalyptic swords and ruthless fire
To self-admitted worms, in the man's heart lay,
Close-gloomed with overtangling bigotries,
A limpid spring of love to his fellow-men;
And from the placid waters of this love
(Which is the holiest any heart may feel,
Being so self-taintless) glad mouths might have drunk
Long balmy draughts of chaste philosophy.
As it was, he made his Christians, Lemuel Lane,
Much as old heathen Hadrian murdered his, —
From a sense of duty.
      Grown beneath his hand,
Lilian, his orphan grandchild, seemed to some
Cold as the silvery ice-flower on a pane, —
A lily blossoming in the frosty air
Of a stern theology's bleak dogmatisms.
Yet to the spring of sweet spontaneous love
Within her grandsire's heart, this girl had found
Some shadowy secret spiritual path,
Some devious daisied byway, hers alone.
And for the coldness of her saintly face,
Whence in smooth waves the pale-gold hair flowed back
Above large serious eyes of starry gray,
Such coldness meant but youth's fresh purity,
Since Lilian's life was like the morning dew
That waits for a sun to thrill its crystal soul!

And even as dew when touched by summer dawn,
She had sense of inward splendor and new warmth
In that sweet hour when Adrian Eliot's smile
First met her look as toward the rose-wound porch
Of Lemuel's cottage he and Alan came
Up through the hollyhocks' red minarets,
One grave as twilight and one merry as noon.

And Adrian, sweeping with astonished eyes
Her beauty, grace by grace discovering it,
Was first to speak; and Lilian loved his voice,
So mellow it rang with manly gentleness.
And while she answered diffidently low,
He noted with mute wonder each choice charm
Of deep bright eyelash, temple tender-veined,
Lip curling upward like an innocent child's,
Clear dainty dimple on the rounded chin,
And wide brow, candid as a stainless heaven!

And now, because he had loved their father well,
Old Lemuel, coming later, staff in hand,
Gave to both guests warm greeting; but his brow
Saddened at fitful whiles amid the talk,
When memories of neglect o'erswept his heart
And thoughts of how his counsel once had served
As trusty guide to Alan's orphaned youth.

Nor could he stay his speech from wandering hints,
Pregnant with sad reproach.   The world was changed,
Yes, mightily changed, he knew, of later years!
Even here in quiet Maine there had been folk
Who had felt the social ripple, as one might say,
Rush broadening from the central turbulence.
Satan was at his own sly tricks again!
(With raps of the stout stick in the withered hand.)
He had bottled that old hell-broth, atheism,
In fine new bottles branded . . . what was the name?
And made this modern monkey-theorist loose
A locust-plague of speculative doubts,
To light on Eden's green faith-watered sward
And leave it desolation!   Ah, for a time
To worship science in place of God might serve,
But soon or late must Ashtoreth and Baal
Be tumbled over in the iniquitous groves
By their own worshippers, while the wrath of Heaven
Thundered along the land . . . " Yet, Alan, lad
(For lad you still must seem to these dim eyes),
I cast no bitterness on your father's son;
I am not your judge — God knows I wish I were!
They say you are grown right scholarly and wise,
Have had the old homestead-library well vamped,
Stored it with books in more than one strange tongue,
And set it round with marble and bronze Voltaires

And half the ungodly eminence of earth
Since Romulus. . . . Well, you come at last to see
The old man your father loved once,— him who thinks
Full often, latterly, that he lives too long
Here in a world where newness fogs the past,
Where that which men call progress, he decay,
Gathers its thickening mildew o'er all faith,
And flaps aloft its impious carrion-wings
Above the white inviolate shape of Christ,
Still gleaming from the imperishable Cross!"

So Lemuel's warm polemic words boiled on,
Throwing off at intervals that ancient fume
Whose strong fanatic must yet stoutly clung
To many a tome on Alan's gloomy shelves,
Classic, mediæval, heathen, Christian sort,
Monkish or Protestant,— whatever shows
Mankind stanch-moored among conservatisms,
Or lighting reverent tripods at the foot
Of some adored idea, whose idol bulk
Clogs the fair fluent stream of onward thought
With might of damming prejudice. Alan heard
As one for whom the words were tales twice-told,
Smiling a little with his sombre lips,
Letting his eyes, more often than he knew,
Wander to Lilian's ethereal face.

But Lilian guessed not of these furtive looks,
For close within the spell of Adrian's voice,
His glowing smile and happy graciousness,
Heart-charmed she sat, and when he had gone, that day,
Heart-charmed she dealt in memories of him still;
Nor seemed herself through many an after-hour,
But moved about with absent eyes of dream,
Oblivious of small household offices,
Or now remembering her forgetfulness
With a rosy blush.
     But on her life there fell
The sudden chilling grief, ere many weeks,
Of her loved grandsire's death: for Lilian stole
At dusk, one evening, to his half-shut door,
And called him, once, again, and yet again,
Till hearing but the clock's quick tick within,
She entered. There, by an open window, sat
Old Lemuel; breezes moved his silver hair;
A Bible on his still knee lay unclosed,
With fluttering leaves; his head, fallen backward, told
Only of calm sleep; on his faded cheek
A sunbeam smote from the dying west . . . vague fear
Laid its cold clasp round Lilian's heart . . . she sprang
Nearer, with a cry . . . through all that night till dawn
She lay and moaned beside the sheeted dead.

Forlornest shadow, with the expiring flame
Of Lemuel's life, wrapt Lilian's. He who went
Had been her last of kindred. Only a life
Deserted thus by one whole perished race
Can truly feel the sacred bond of blood!
And he, the dead man, though he had often seemed
In other eyes a rigorous guard enough,
A seraph-martinet, at the gate of Heaven,
In hers wore tenderer traits; for she had heard
Humanity's full-pulsed heart beat forcefully
Below the corselet of this paladin saint.
Loud-roared were his sulphureous prophecies
On Sabbath morns, yet often afterward,
She lingering by his arm-chair, he would drop
In silence on her curls, with delicate touch,
Benedictions. "Ah, I knew him, only I,"
She sobbed to the kind neighbors when they came.
"I had his honey, if others felt his sting.
I loved him, knowing him what he was . . . and now
I am kinless and alone!"
      But Lilian found
Another trouble thwarting her young life;
For with the old preacher died his wage, and she,
Left with no guard against the fangs of want
Save the frail needle she so deftly plied,
Fought with proud plaintless quiet her brave fight

For bread. And now, on a certain eve, it fell,
While passing homeward in the dubious blue
Of dusk to the village outskirts, quick of step
(Her gold hair lovelier for her darksome gear,
Her pale face glimmering paler), that she met
Adrian, and that with courtly gentleness,
Passing, he held a moment in his own
Her tremulous hand. "I came in search of you,"
He murmured; "at your door I left my horse;
They had told me you would take this path . . . I learned
But lately that your home was changed." Therewith,
Dropping her hand, he walked at Lilian's side,
Below the outflowering stars, in the cool dusk.

And Adrian further said, in gentlest way,
"You have need of help; your grandsire was well-loved
Of our dead father. Alan and myself
Would hold it precious privilege to make
Your burden lighter for you . . . Sanction us!"
And Lilian answered, with an upward look
And starrier from those great gray eyes of hers
Full into Adrian's own: "I give you thanks.
But see, I am decent-clad and well to do;
I have need of neither lodgement, clothes, nor bread.
Work brings me all. It is my amulet, work,
And guards me from myself; for one's own thoughts

Are bitter visitants to a life that moves
Kinless, alone, through this unpitying world!"

"Nay, kinless, if you will," said Adrian then,
Impetuously, " but therefore not alone!"
His voice for an instant shook with one rich throb
Of feeling. Lilian's fluttered heart stood still,
But her deep shining eyes irresistibly
Were lifted up toward his, and there she read . . .
She knew not what; and o'er the shadowy land
A sweet wild wind, that sprang from the summer sea
And smelt of its waves, came floating; and this wind
Bore to the ears of Lilian's soul a sound
Like trilling tinkles of many silver bells,
Joy-bells, and to her soul's pure lips it bore
A draught of that strange rich unearthly wine
Whose mellowing grape has bathed a magic globe
In sunlight of Hesperian valleylands!

The heavens had long been whitened with their stars
When Adrian at the homestead-gate, that night,
Drew rein. And many another night he walked
With Lilian while the summer lived, nor thought
If Alan's brows were gloomier, or its word
Less frequent on the reticent scholar's lip.
For love, first love, that sweet blithe torch-bearer,

Had waved his rosy torch through Adrian's soul,
Till every mood of it henceforth was clad
In gracious glory, and he beheld the world
With altered eye. The summer suns, for him,
Sank westward with a kinglier gorgeousness,
The daisy rocked to breeze of balmier touch,
And richlier orbed in reaches of dim pearl,
Nightly chaste Hesper trembled.
                                Through these days
An agony gnawed Alan Eliot's heart,
Though his brother dreamed it not. For since the hour
When Lilian stood upon the rose-wound porch,
Meeting himself and Adrian, Alan's thought
Had dwelt with secret fire of growing love
On her bright shape; yet he had found this love
As strange a guest within his studious life
As a laughing child-face in some solemn vault.
Never till now he had known what live love meant,
Never till now had seen its fleshly form,
But always watched it, from cold critic heights,
In some Greek statuesque Æschylean way,
Glide as a ghost amid the ghostly past.

But now its influence dragged him from his books,
Hollowed his faded cheek and glazed his eye,
And sent him wandering through the summer lands,

Goaded by sharp shame; for he had willed, this man,
Always to sit aloof, exemptedly,
Like a Trojan elder on the Scæan tower,
And view that battle of souls, humanity,
With contemplating unparticipant look.
But a sudden shaft of fight had struck him down,
Mocking the arrogance that dared to claim
It might elude the ineludible doom
And miss the big wounds and deep aches of life,
Withdrawn in calms of intellectual ease.

Yet still he stoutly grasped the stubborn hope
That grave self-counsels would avail at last
Balsamically to assuage this hurt.
He swore that he would never look again,
Of his free act, on Lilian's face; he swore
To tear this folly of feeling like a weed
From where it thrust such violative root.
And now for some brief while the man's great will
Seemed possible victor. With grim lips compressed,
Like one who sets heel on a serpent's head,
He whispered to his own strange heart, "I win."
Then came the abrupt news of old Lemuel's death. . . .
He must not, he nor Adrian, miss to stand
At burial of their father's trusted friend. . . .
And so the brothers went, and Lilian's face,

With all its mute pale pathos, touched his soul,
O'erthrowing his imperious resolve,
Unmanacling his passion, ruining all
The work of weeks. And Adrian, who had known
Nothing before, knew nothing now, but thought
His brother led by whim or heed of health
To roam for hours on long and lonely tramps.
Longer they grew, and less could study lure
The uneasy mind as new days glided on.
But now he had made avowal to himself,
Strange lover that he was, of full defeat.
First would he let one decorous mourning-month
Elapse, and then his wooing in good truth
Frankly should open. "I have failed," he said,
"I am despicably weak;" yet while he spoke
A strong joy trembled in his breast, a light
As of some pure divine dawn seemed to make
His future wealthful with surpassing hope,
And vaguely on his haughty heart there fell
Delicious realization of how love
Finds in humility its own best pride,
And from ecstatic self-abasement plucks
A purple dignity.   In these same hours
It fell that Adrian from some village folk,
Riding one day past doors he had known a boy,

Learned of young Lilian's poverty and how
She had fought with want. In conference, that night,
Between himself and Alan it was planned
That Adrian should make offer of large help,
But delicately, not in way to wound.
And Adrian, little dreaming of the snare
Latent in those deep amiable eyes,
With Lilian had held converse, as we know.
And often again they met, and made at last
Betrayal and confession absolute,
Either to either, of undying love!
And Alan, ignorant of these happy trysts,
Was murmuring to himself, "The time is ripe,"
When suddenly, a thunderbolt of shock,
The appalling truth leapt forth and struck him dumb.

For Adrian joined him in a seaward walk,
One vaporous morning when the dewy leaves
Were garbed in gaudy omen of their death.
Autumn, now boldly dominant again,
Had woven her brilliant spells about the trees
And touched the distances with hazier blue,
Or brought the sweetly querulous winds from south
To search for the ruined rose they never found.
And then, with glad awakening from grave dreams
Of the flown summer, she had made her skies

Clear-cold, her breezes amply resonant,
Her flaky and rolling clouds a power to shed
Long tracts of shadow across the glowing slopes.
And then she had fallen to sleep again for days,
And through her dreams the bland winds moved once
 more.

On such a languid morn the brothers went
By pastoral ways toward the misty sea.
A withering splendor of slim golden-rods
Plumed many a knoll, and rich imperial tints
Yet lingered in the clustering aster-sprays.
The encrimsoned sumachs lifted garnet knots
Of fruitage, and a murmurous maple-grove
Blazed as with blended scarlets, pinks and golds
Of some thick gaudy stuff from Orient looms.
Those plenteous vines, the ivies of our west,
Wrapt with their vivid and luxurious red
The yellowing hickory's trunk or the dark fringe
Of oval cedars; heavy from lithe stems
Drooped the black lustrous beads of the elder-flower,
And roseate on their prickly girandoles
Burned the pale delicate thistles like dim flames.
Faint lazy airs went wandering o'er the land,
Rustling the brittle pomp of low-fallen leaves,
And at the pale sky's limit, velvet-soft,
One stagnant ring of smoky purple drowsed.

And now it was that Adrian spoke, low-voiced,
Of how deep love had strengthened in his life
To sweet vitality through these late weeks.
And yet he had named no name when Alan said:
"What, boy! At your age? . . . You are young to bear
This weightsome yoke you talk so glibly of.
Nay, now, be sure that what you take for gold,
True passionate gold, will turn, some future day,
Illusory glitter, transient flash of whim."
Then Adrian answered: "Alan, I should shame
To give so noble a girl so light a love!
You know her ill indeed, or you would know
How whitely beams among all kindred sort
Her spirit, a holy lamp of womanhood!
And yet you have beheld her face ere this,
For she is Lilian Lane, by Lemuel's death
Left poor and kinless, though incapable
To lean on any staff but brave self-help."

So Adrian proudly yet unwittingly
Spoke, and on Alan Eliot's soul there fell
The darkness of an anguish unforeseen,
Blackening the misty waters that he neared.

And Adrian further spoke of Lilian's love,
The rapture of remembrance blinding him

To Alan's fiery eyes and livid lips,
Both partly hidden from his own bright look.
" She is all sweet golden fealty and trust,"
He murmured; then, with lightsome laughter, said:
" But, Alan, you will smile when you have seen
The lofty pedestal she thrones me on!
I am hero, prince, king, demigod to her,
Dear Lilian!" . . . And in Alan a wild voice
Was mutely crying: " O God! must I walk here
Beside this insolent urchin-thief who robs
My future of all hope, yet say no word?"

And still within the man tyrannic pride
Put vetoing silence on his mouth, and wove
A gradual mask about his tell-tale face,
And nerved him potently, erewhile, to speak
With tranquil voice and unimpassioned mien,
Of Adrian's love to Adrian. Hot flame raged
Below his calmness, yet it raged unseen;
Hot curses leapt to his lips, but did not pass;
He smiled full often, though he had liefer groan,
Even laughed once, with superb hypocrisy;
So mighty a thing is pride in some men's souls.

But when he had escaped from Adrian's sight,
Close-shut within the cloistral library

That teemed with memories of his peaceful past,
Then fiercely, in one burst of vehemence,
His great pain spoke aloud. He seemed to strike
Abruptly against a future that forbade
All prescience, dumb as a great bolted door!
How must it fare with him in after time?
How might he live, thus maimed by a crushing blow?
Ah, fool, to have lingered, lingered! Adrian's hand
Had plucked from out the field this daisy-star
For which he had waited in his egotism,
So certain, with insensate certainty,
That the mere wanting its pale fragile bloom
Ordained possession! Had he strength to play
His needed rôle of smooth serenity
When the hour should come for clasping with his own
Lilian's complaisant hand, while wishing her
All earthly happiness in Adrian's love?
"Ah, how I have served as puppet," Alan moaned,
"For problematic and inscrutable fate!
O fearful force of what we name events!
Who dares to babble and prate of human will?
Nay, nay, we are all mere straws upon the brook,
Leaves in the wind, who dream we sail or fly
Whither each pleases, yet are borne along
Obedient always to some mighty law!
We smile: it is a part of the awful scheme!

We weep: some long vast sequence gains a link!
And whence we move and toward what final bourne
We know not, burrowing sightless through the dark,
Like moles! ... "
     He hugged this baleful fatalism
For days, and from its darkness gathered light,
As one that wins from a rank noisome herb
The salve of healing; and he attained at length
Some sort of inward peace below a mask
Of outward calm, ere Lilian looked on him
And let his hand press hers with firm cool touch.
Then gravely but with easeful grace he said:
"Believe me, Adrian's choice of wife and mine
Of sister blend in happiest accord."
But Adrian, who stood near, called laughingly:
"Come, seal that pretty sentiment with a kiss!"
Then soon did Lilian feel against her brow
Two lips of ice, and shivering ill could choke
Back into silence an affrighted cry. . . .

That night no sleep touched Alan Eliot's brain.
That night, and many another night, he lay
As wakeful as the turbulent autumn winds
That shook the towering pines on the chill lawns
And spoke the language of his own despair!
And many a day the solemn library

Knew not his presence, but for hours he sat
Near a stern lonesome cliff whose bold wall verged
A tongue of bleak precipitous coastland, set
Jaggedly seaward, well aloof from home.

Now, under this wild cliff-line, as it chanced,
The silver chisels of the sea had wrought
A shallow cave, lined thick with beaded kelp.
But overhead the abrupt height backward fell,
And in the hollow, as though half-poised in air,
Jutted from out a bed of stolid earth
One ponderous rounded boulder that had hung
Above the cave for immemorial years.
To Alan, through his boyhood, this quaint cave
Had ever seemed a thing of wondrous craft;
He had dreamed, in other days, that when the tide
Had filled its weedy void with foamful surge,
Here might some lissome gold-haired mermaid dwell,
Singing rich passionate songs on summer nights
To her gold lute; for weeks no foot save his
Would haunt the bald acclivities above
Or the drab sands beneath, so drearily
Was this bleak shore to its own bleakness left.
But once, as Alan faithfully recalled,
His father and himself had wandered here
Below the boulder, close against the cave;

And Alan's father musingly had said,
Not knowing if Alan heard, or caring not,
"Our stormy winters, with their vast sea-shocks,
Will drag that stone, one day, from where it clings."

Since then much earth had left the beetling stone,
But still it hung; and now, on a dull eve,
While Alan stared at the dull iron sea,
Sharp rain from an iron heaven fell chillingly
And drove him homeward in the teeth of the wind,
Shivering; and clear through one long fretful week,
Made captive by the incessant rain, he bode
Within the house; but Adrian braved, each day,
Boreas in all his maddest moods to leave
The lover's kiss on Lilian's lifted mouth.
And Alan, knowing of where he went, would feel
New pangs of infinite envy; and the peace
That latterly had ruled him disappeared,
Imperative unrest replacing it,
And dark wild fits when Adrian's face or voice,
Met suddenly, made him ache with hate.
       Not lost
On Adrian was the sullen word or look.
For often his brother's mien would startle him,
And set him wondering "What can ail the man?"
And soon within his large and generous heart

Adrian mused sweetly: "Is he angered, then?
Perchance he has cause for anger: what know I?
Perchance I may have wounded him with depth
By some light act; for he is wise and good,
Learned beyond many a one deemed scholarly,
And shrewd in worldly ways though shunning them.
So were it best to frankly ask my fault,
And being assured of that, frankly to ask
His pardon."
    On the morn that Adrian made
This high and pure resolve, the prisoning rain
In volumes of dark vapor densely rolled
Eastward and left the deep vast dome of heaven
With wintry pearl in its cold limpid blue.
And from the window of his room, that day,
It chanced that Adrian saw his brother go
(A dark tall shape, clear-seen in frosty air)
Forth where the distant promontory loomed.
And Adrian followed, saying inwardly:
"Now is my time. There will I meet with him
As though by accident, and ask my fault."

Meanwhile with bowed head, with determined step
And thoughts that fed on darkness, Alan passed
Right to the cliff's gray edge. The tide was low,
And not the loftiest wave that smote the beach

Could slip its rapid sheet of stealthy foam
Farther than midway of the sand's brown floor.
And now while Alan from the sheer cliff watched
The exultant and illimitable glow
Of autumn ocean, suddenly a bird
Soared from beneath him with one husky scream,
And near the spot whence the wild thing had leapt,
Amazed he looked on Adrian, who in turn
Gazed at the egress of the cave as one
Whom boyish memory quite enthralls; and soon,
Drawn by this power of memory to explore
The weedy and darksome grotto, Adrian
Entered it, vanishing from him who watched.

Then stole a ghastly thought through Alan's mind
While he beheld the great o'erbrowing stone,
And noted how the wash of recent rains
Had channelled its engirding earth and sent
Huge flakes below.... "One vigorous push," he thought,
"Just at the proper moment, when the boy
Emerges thence ... a single vigorous push,
And who shall say if the great stone, quite loosed,
Would tumble not to the underlying shore?"
So flashed the hideous thought through Alan's brain.
But the next instant, with astounded sight,
As though the horrid shadow of his own dream

Had suddenly grown substance, he discerned
The lapsing of moist earth-clods round the stone,
Saw it sink slowly downward and then hang
Motionless, and at length with monstrous lurch
Fall crashing and thundering shoreward from the cliff.

Dizzied and horror-chilled he stood awhile,
Then dropped his look to where the vast mass lay.
The cave no more was visible; its mouth
Was sealed with a dread seal that one man's strength
Were powerless to dissever as the touch
From ripple of risen tide were powerless.
And he who had gone within stood sepulchred,
Breathing dense darkness through his very blood,
Trapped in a fastness fronting dangerous reefs
That scared away all chance of aiding sails,
While imminent cliff and bouldered shore might meet
For long bluff windy days no visitant
Save some shrill feathered waif of the air and sea.

Such thought sprang up like fire in Alan's breast . . .
"And yet, by a mercy," cried his spirit, "fate
Allots that you shall see the dreadful sight!
Deliverance breathes in you! Go, shriek to him
Instantly through that great entombing mass
That you, his brother, have seen all! Cry forth:

'Be of good cheer. You are safe as though you heard
Already scores of hands wrench, pry, and pierce!'
Haste! go to him now! Each minute of duress
Is big with torture ere he knows you near!
Let sixty such wild minutes clustering make
An hour, and liberty might find the man
With horror-whitened hair and gibbering lips!"

Already Alan Eliot bent his steps
Down toward the cumbered cave; already, too,
His face was softening, and a piteous light
Burned in his gaze; eager to save he looked,
Eager to melt by a cry of Adrian's name
The trance of mortal fear that now must wrap
His brother's heart.
     Then suddenly all changed.
He paused beside a rough declivity,
Sank down in trembling heap, bowed his head low,
And stared with eyes of spectral fixity
At nothing; then with dull strange hollow voice
He spoke, yet doubtless knew not if he spoke,
Muttering:
   "I saw, I know it! I alone!
The man I have loathed as we loathe all that bars
Clear path toward those attainments we most love,
Waits for my will to crush him or to save!

My will?   But will is choice between two acts,
And choice is minion of desire.   Free will!
Pah! men with catchwords flatter their own fates!
Effect forever spaniels at the heel
Of cause; one mood begets the next; and we,
Powerless to shape two simultaneous deeds,
Are choiceless through apparent power of choice.
What cause now governs me, to what effect?
Love's hand, grown steel, drags me to slake my hate!
Within the unmeasured deeps of my own love
I am weak as some stray meteor wildly flung
Through starry and dark-blue altitudes of night,
Whither it knows not, knowing alone it serves
The radiant rapid slave of sovereign law.
So I serve now!   Let Adrian die! ..."
                                          The words
Faltered upon his blanched lips, then; he hid
His low face wholly from the sun, with hands
That showed the tremor storming his bowed frame.
He thought of Adrian sweating icy sweat
There in the awful bondage of his tomb.
He felt the agony, the keen despair
Of hours immense as years within that cave,
Black terrible hours of gropings and vain cries
That filled with fearful hoarseness the rasped throat
And tinged with blood the blind dilated eye.

He loathed himself that even his passing thought
Should take this murderous and infernal shape.
To his feet he sprang, sped downward a brief space,
And waved both arms high, as in helpful sign . . .
Then, with abrupt restraint, he paused once more.
His devil had caught him now in mastering grip;
He clenched both hands to a knot, smiled a set smile,
Breathed hard, the blank look in his eyes again,
And then, at mad precipitate break-neck speed,
Fled from the shore. . . .
     Up the drab sands the surf
With affluent or with refluent motion swung;
Dim veils of vapor, shreds of the late wrack,
Moved ghostly across the lucid blue of heaven;
The austere cliffs bathed their rude granitic might
In the bold windy glow of the fresh morn,
And if above splashed waves or hurrying breeze,
Any vague strange cry haunted that far place,
Only the fleet gull heard it, glimmering past,
Or the wild white hawk on the jutting crag.

 . . . . . .

After three days a clouded morning brought
Lilian, alarmed and pale, to Alan's doors.
Pale and of marble calmness, Alan met
Her eager questions. No, he had heard, himself,
Nothing of Adrian, seen no trace of him,

Since, at an early hour, three morns ago,
His brother had departed, whither bound
He knew not, nor could find a soul that knew.
Then Lilian uttered a great plaintive cry.
" Missing three days! Three days!" A querulous fear
Shrilled in her voice. "Three days! Yet have you made
No effort to discover if any harm
Has reached him?" "Nay," said Alan, colder-voiced,
" I have done the best I knew, and should have gone
This day to inquire of you concerning him,
Had you not sought me." Now poor Lilian's eyes
Glittered in tears. " I have been to blame," she cried,
" For thus impetuously chiding you!"
She caught his hand . . . then, shivering as from pain,
Dropt it because its coldness pierced her heart.

The slow inevitable morrows came,
Widened their weeks to months immutably,
Their months to a year. Pangs of surpassing grief
Had racked poor Lilian, and her hope had ceased
Either that Adrian lived or that the dark
Mystery of his vanishment would clear.
And Alan now and then would visit her
Throughout this time; solemn as death their talks,
Filled with low-murmured reference to the lost.
And often against her will would Lilian show,

In that white way of still persistent tears,
How a hurt heart will bleed.   So one year went.

But in the year that followed Adrian's loss
It fell, one day, that Alan suddenly told
Lilian of his great love.   For while they sat
Near the broad hearth where a big lurid log
Brightened its dreamy red as the blue dusk
Of drear December deepened, Alan spoke
His passion, saying, "I love you, Lilian—
I love you from my soul!   God knows I do!"
Strongly those grave words rang from his grave lips.
And Lilian trembled, there in the dim room,
Awed by the revelation of this love
Undreamed of till it flashed upon her now
From out the man's cold sombreness, as when
A cavernous cloud is drenched with elfin fire
For an instant, while it hangs in breezeless gloom,
And all its inward haunts of coast, peak, glen,
Viewed fleetingly, a new weird world in air,
Glimmer to die; but as they die we have gazed
Into the cloud's wild soul: even thus with her,
Who seemed to have seen through Alan Eliot's soul.

Then she rose up and answered with slow words:
"I wonder you should tell me of such love!"

And said no more, but stole away from him,
Leaving him quite alone in the dim room, —
With ghastly firelit face, dark-shining eyes,
Mouth saturnine and rigid-folded arms.

. . . .

They who abode with Alan in the old house
Where now he lived the old life of grim recluse,
Whispered that they had heard, through these same
      months,
Keen cries or deep groans, in the middle night,
From Alan's chamber echoing; and once
A wrinkled wreck of woman, she who served
As Alan's trusted nurse long years before,
Declared that going aloft to bed, one night,
She had met her master roaming the great hall,
And by the light of her dim lamp had seen
That he was clad as though of mind to fare
Into the sharp dark out of doors; but soon
She had seen, moreover, from his vacant face,
His frigid sightless look, his stiff strange walk,
That the man slept, and crying had wakened him;
And though he had borne himself in mindless way
When first awake, muttering and gesturing,
He presently became his old stern self,
Thanked her who roused him, and so passed to bed.

. . . .

Though Lilian fled from Alan on that day
When, in the firelit dusk, he told his love,
She formed no hard resolve to break with him;
But rather, when he came again, by signs
Her sensitive face made easy to discern
He read her pity and was ill-pleased with it,
Yet murmured to his heart that pity and love
Were often each to each like sire to child.
So more weeks passed, and Alan grew again
Lilian's close friend, her constant visitor.
And Lilian, whose girl-eyes had always seen
Learning at distance, like some town remote
That crowds a mist of towers against the blue,
Seemed with this man, by gradual paths of talk,
To wander nearer, till the glimmering grace
Of column, frieze and stately portico
From dim neutrality gleamed clear of shape.
And he could soften his voice with sweet accords,
Could soften his lean cold face, too, when with her,
And deft of phrase he was, by fluent tricks
That knew to hide the difficult prongs of fact
In all he uttered, as fleet streams will hide
With glassy oversweep some bulging stone.
Richly his dark eyes flashed, too, now and then,
And voice and eyes told Lilian more than once
Things that she found it meagre joy to know,

While thrilled with growing pleasure when she thought
"This man, so intellectually a man,
So finelier-fashioned both in mind and heart
Than other men, loves me who am cultureless,
Even ignorant."   So the weeks went, and so
Alan still wooed, and after many days
Again he avowed his passion fervently,
And Lilian answered, "Nay, I am not worth
Such love as yours!" (and while she spoke her breast
Was stirred with no sweet warmth, and equably
Throbbed her calm pulse;) "but it is honor, still,
To have had this high love proffered." . . . Then he
       spoke,
Persuasively because of his vast love,
And in a little while he had won his cause,
And girded her with worshipping arms, and put
His lips against her brow. . . . But quickly then,
Shivering she writhed from out his close embrace,
And crying aloud yet incoherently,
Sank on a couch, and with palm-shaded face
Burst into sobs.   And bending over her,
Alan put question, "Lilian, what is this?" . . .
At first she would not answer, but at last
With face yet hid she moaned in plaintive way,
As though to herself, " Now am I sure indeed
That Adrian lives not, for I have seen his ghost!"

And Alan Eliot, with fear-whitened cheek,
Started at this, then hastily went out
Into the cool Spring twilight where aloft
Hung a wan moon whose globe caught paler fire
As the day darkened.   Lowered was his face,
But those who passed him, had they looked on it,
Would then have seen how all its lineaments
Had grown one horror. . . .

     Simply these were wed
In a few weeks, and Alan Eliot gained
That which he had desired so boundlessly,
Yet gained it not, since Lilian, while she strove
To play her wifely part in wifeliest way,
Left from it that intangible delight
Which is to woman's hand-clasp, smile or kiss
As odor unto flower.   She could not feign
That higher holier feeling, and he saw
Both that she tried and that she failed outright;
And drearily, or sometimes passionately,
Or sometimes filled with haunting fear, he said
All low to himself, in guilty whisper, then:
" The dead man stands between us . . ."

      Gloomier grown,
When now their days of honeymoon were fled,
He yet would show for Lilian the same love
As always, though with feverish outbursts broken,

Or touched, it might be, with sharp petulance
No sooner shown than sternly self-condemned.
But now it fell that Lilian altered much,
Given to long gazings at her husband's face
When he observed her not, or, if he marked,
Prone to avert her eyes bewilderedly,
Like one surprised in some delinquent deed.
And Alan, wondering, questioned of himself
Wherefore this curious change had risen, and soon
Saw other signs in Lilian that aroused
Wonder, anxiety, he knew not what. . . .

One night, when all the house was deadly still,
And wholly dark, and clocks from room to room
Struck the small hours in doleful muffled throbs,
There went forth to the starlight of the lawn
A human shape, arrayed for open night.
Now this was Alan Eliot that went forth;
And though he walked with firm and even pace,
He slept. . . .
   The heavens looked one pale crust of stars,
The journeying breeze blew suave with latter May,
And night hung sparkling o'er the drowsy sea.

Out toward the tongue of bleak precipitous land
Whose horrid secret he and no man else

Had known since fell that huge entombing rock,
Went Alan, and in wondrous manner found,
Although he slept, the old egress of the cave,
Still barred with the old enormous boulder. Here
He paused on sands left bare from fallen tides,
And laying both hands on the boulder, said,
With voice so hollow as to seem not his:
"Adrian, I saw it fall and shut you in!
I saw it fall, and now I hurry away
For help. . . . What hideous thought was that? No, no!
I hurry away for help! Keep Lilian's love! . . .
Turn murderer? — steep myself in loathsome crime? —
I, Alan Eliot, I who drank so deep
Of knowledge! I, who have seen the roots of life
Coiling their toughness down amid the dark
Of the Unknowable, and traced the streams
Of good and evil to their uttermost urns, —
I sink like this in vulgar mire of sin,
And all for a fern-frail creature, one slight girl!
No! no! say what you please, philosophy;
Man's will is wholly free will; crime is crime,
Not a mere malady of the brain. We stand,
Whether God cares or not, for all our deeds
Accountable in sight of our own souls.
No! no! hark, Adrian, brother Adrian!
The Adrian that I bore, a little lad,

Here on these shoulders, hark! ... I hurry away
For help. ..."

    A something plucked his sleeve and woke
Alan; the starlight showed a livid face,
Lilian's; for she had followed him by stealth,
Knowing he slept; and now she had heard his words
That flashed their terrible torch on other words,
Dull mutterings heard while she in other nights
Had lain beside him. Never woman born
Was gentlier fashioned through and through her soul
Than Lilian; but her lovely face was now
Imperious, her meek eyes were fired with hate.
Large loomed her stature by the starlit sea,
For untold wrath possessed her, and a sense
Of outrage in its grief-born might sublime.
And now her voice rang hoarsely on the night,
A voice where love met loathing, and where, too,
Transcendent anguish dashed itself on speech.

"God tears from all this horror the veil at last!
I see you now the vile mean thing you are,
Monster abominable, hypocrite
Supreme! ... Ah, Heaven, though I was reared to trust
God utterly, my spirit falters now
In faith toward that high hand which seems to lay
Such heavy curse upon it; for I feel

My whole self, body and soul, at this wild hour,
One blackness of pollution from your love!
How to your own foul heart you must have laughed,
Remembering that through pity I wedded you!
What wonder Adrian left the dark of death
To warn me, when your first audacious kiss
Laid its unguessed corruption on my brow?
He should have struck you a great vengeful blow
Before your impious arms dared clasp this neck!
Oh, my lost Adrian, my one only love,
'T is woe enough to learn your fearful fate,
But ah, worse woe that I have wived with him
Whose unconjectured baseness let you die!
How could the very stone of your dread tomb
Not render you in mercy back to light?
How could the winds not bear me as they went
Echoes of your mad summons, or the sea
Not sap the bases of your ghastly tomb?"

She paused, and in the silence that ensued,
He heard her laboring breath sound short and strong.

" But now if I seem sport for a whim of God,
Oh, rest sure, Alan Eliot, none the less,
That somewhere lurks the atonement of your sin,
Stretched like the waiting rack that wrings men's frames.

I love the old savage creed my grandsire taught,
The creed of endless penance in hot hell, —
Yes, love it now, though once I hated it!
From this dark hour I yearn to test its truth, —
To feel that you in torment exquisite
Eternally shall writhe!   Oh, if my curse
Can send you swiftlier to that agony,
Then hear me, Thou that calling of old to Cain,
Didst ask of him a brother!   May this man,
For howsoever long he bides on earth,
Feel always round his heart a hand of steel
That slowly tears it from his breast, and yet
Never so tears it; and may mighty pangs
Of self-contempt assail and crush him down!
May deadly dreams clasp clammy hands with him
In the dusk halls of slumber, till he wakes
With shuddering cry and cold sweat-beaded skin!
May all his life till death be misery,
And all his after-life infinitude
Of pain!   O God, may this man crawl to death
Panting for draughts of it yet find worse thirst,
Even as a soldier on some battle-field
May drag his bleeding gashes toward what looks
A stream's dear edge, and groaning thankfully,
With drought-cracked lips drink in sun-blistered clay!"

. . . .

Long ere she ceased he had covered with both hands
His face. And now between a shriek and sob
Her fierce words ended, and she dashed away,
Flying in madness of despair to friends
That dwelt amid the village: these she found,
Rousing them up from sleep and thrilling them
With her dark story; some believed it not,
But thought she raved, so frantic was her mien.

Yet with the morrow's light her better self
Returned, and as a devil exorcised,
Her spirit of curseful vengeance passed away.

But no smile ever touched her gentle face,
From this until the hour, ten full years thence,
That saw her die; and all her lovely hair,
After that wild night by the starlit sea,
Was white as with the snows of seventy years.

Yet through her life thenceforward precious peace
Touched her with soft remedial balm; she gained
Sweet quiet and the inestimable joy
Of pardoning him who wrought her such vast harm.
For at the last calm moment of her life,
A great smile lit her lips, and "Long ago,"
She said, "I have forgiven him everything. . . .

And if he lives on earth I would he knew
That dying I have forgiven him everything. . . .
And if he is dead, may God be merciful
A little more to him because of this,
That Lilian Lane forgives him everything!"
Then once she murmured "Adrian," and so died.

Yet though 't is years since her poor bruised soul went,
No human eye, from that dire night till now,
Has knowingly seen Alan Eliot's face.
If he be live or dead it is not known;
A mystery darker than young Adrian's tomb
Shadows him, and the old homestead, standing yet,
Hears through its empty chambers the long roar
Of winter ocean, or when summer blooms,
Looks from its dusty and cobwebbed panes to see
The rank grass deepen down the untended lawn,
Or on the untraversed paths green giant weeds
Throng insolent, and then rot themselves away.

THE REPUBLIC.

*Read before the Phi Beta Kappa Society of Harvard College,
June, 1880.*

I.

REPUBLIC, made at length
    Splendid for stately strength,
O thou at once our glory and hope and pride,
Hear us, for at thy knee
Gathering, we thrill to be
Children of those that in thy lordly cause once died!
Thou wert an ungrown power, in that far time
Of eager patriots, dying for the right;
But now, with mien imperial and sublime,
No more a youngling weak and slight,
Thou standest, viewed by many a neighbor clime,
Clothed with a terrible majesty like light,
Awful yet strangely lovely in thy maiden might!

II.

Now past its hundredth year,
Thy green youth bursts its bud,

Aloe-like blossoming into beauteous flower;
A bloom whose petals clear
Gleam with no stains of blood
From slaughterous Malvern's rout or hot Antietam's
  hour.
All memories now of those distracted years
Are swept from thy sweet name,
And lo, the pureness of thy virginal fame
Radiantly white appears,
Washed clean from any shadow of soiling blame
By pitiful and penitential tears!
From palm-plumed lands that tropic water laves
To where the Atlantic hurls on rugged Maine
The cold green turbulence of his massive waves,
Alike to South and North the unnumbered slain
Speak with soft eloquence of one common pain,
In the mute pathos of their multitudinous graves!

III.

There are who name thee with a mournful sigh,
Our country, murmuring how that chaste ideal
Which great-souled dreamers loved in days gone by,
Is now substantiate in this earthy real!
These point to many a fraud and loathsome lie;
To ignorance throned where wisdom's word should rule;
To gold's insatiate lust,

Or bribery's acrid poison, rotting trust,
Till the pure statesman turns the vulgar lobbyist's tool;
To liberty in the slanderer's lawless pen;
Equality in the plutocrat's curled lip,
And in the plunderous leagues of public men
Fraternity's millennial fellowship!
These question where our leaders live,
Loftily representative,
Free in their reverent vassalage to right;
Not making high responsibilities don
The liveried menial's plight;
Not following where brute avarice may bid,
That while their fleeting terms of power lapse on,
Gross personal booty may be well increased,—
Like lacqueys among their master's pantries hid,
Guzzling the wine-lees of the feast!
And other cavillers, honestly enough,
Ask if our popular order, civic worth,
The old strong heroic stuff,
Be evident in this regretful dearth,
While all the intrigues of greedy railroad kings
With steam are symbolling their own pompous puff,
Illusory credit, light repute on earth,
And virtues flung to the winds like weightless things!
Yet others ask what welfare may abide
In desolate Southern homes where famine's creep

Grows stealthier toward the final leap;
Where rusts the unnoted implement beside
The ungathered harvest's growth,
And where the famishing negro is not loath,
With poor brain fed on its new blood-bought pride,
To loll in his emancipated sloth!

IV.

Ah, cavillers, wherefore gaze
Only upon the shadow of that dear shape,
Our bright Republic, heir of the unborn days,
Nor look toward where the godlike tresses drape
A brow of luminous majesty and eyes
Unfathomable as deeps of dawn-bathed skies?
Nay, who shall solve the awful riddle of time?
The veil of the inmost temple who shall rend?
If discords break the solemn centuries' chime,
Why may not these, even these, divinely blend
Toward some serene and unimagined end,
To breathe some grander harmony that our ear
May no more hear
Than some slight shell, pale waif of the outer tide
Tossed lightly upon some shore,
Down in its fragile roseate whorl may hide
The resonance of all ocean's haughty roar!
Nay, cavillers, for a moment pause . . .

Does liberty shine less brilliantly to-day
Because within man's breast that spark of the god
Would seem to prophesy its own decay?
Is slavery less of sacrilege because
His freedom finds the slave an indolent clod?
Or peace less beautiful because men still slay?
Ah! let us not forget
That the effort once to grandly do is more
Than myriads of achievements aimed less high;
And that when a people's purpose hath been set
Toward some end nobler yet,
Some loftier goal of good unsought before,
Then deeds and words that cannot utterly die
Leap into life with a flash whence men are shown
Eternal Truth calm-browed on her eternal throne!

V.

America, thou art not to blame
If slow humanity crawls and will not run
Toward lands more golden, that the wealthful sun
Of freedom richlier warms and shines upon!
America, in thy name
The best that men can do this hour is done!
Of progress in its onward flight
Thine are the sinewy fearless eagle-wings;
Thou art the foremost in the world's wide fight

For royaller royalties than fleshly kings.
On Europe, numbed with tyranny's cold spell,
The auroral light of thy great sunrise fell,
And lo, as when some glacial polar sea
Is smitten of Spring down all its torpid deep,
And through it mighty lengthening fissures creep,
Or ominous rumbling throes begin to be,
So in the Old World's long-frozen breast awoke
Desires that seemed at first of faint degree,
But now become desires no power can choke
Till the ancient East like the young West is free!
Yet not the mad mob, furious to be fed,
Groaning wild violent words of priest and tax,
Not flaming palaces, nor streets clogged with dead,
Nor white throats bared below the pitiless axe,
Not these, O liberty, are the potent means
Wherewith thy reverend cause is profited.
Thou valuest more than slaughtered kings and queens
The slaying of baser passions in men's blood;
And more than jewelled crowns being flung in mud,
The glitter of self-love spurned by noble feet.
More than all ruinous fire to thee is sweet
That holy and never-flickering flame which feeds
Not on cathedral-spires nor monkish bones,
Nor fragments broken away from gilded thrones,
But whose pure outflow burns intense

With patient charity's myrrh and frankincense
And the rich sacred fuel of chaste unselfish deeds!

VI.

For liberty, though her range be vastly wide,
Still moves in glorious orbit round some might
Unknowable, whose colossal satellite
She is and must perpetually abide.
That which we call being free is but to say
That we are free to obey, —
That we are free to adore, to reverence right!
Once swerve from that sublimer statelier way,
Once break the golden gyves of self-control,
And lo, a desolate freedom finds the soul,
A broad captivity whose realm begins
Where folly's vaporous air holds blinding sway,
But whose dark distance its wild boundary wins
Among the appalling glooms of unrestricted sins!

VII.

So dreamed and taught the old noble Greeks,
Haters of manacle and yoke,
Dwellers on wisdom's mountain-peaks,
They that such grand philosophy spoke,
Making their nation's heart beat such magnificent stroke!
Even so they taught and dreamed,

While Athens, that clear lily of freedom, rose
A glorious martial flower
Where the blue Ægean gleamed,
With precious odors flowing across the world
From petals whiter than Olympian snows!
But lo, in an evil hour,
To the dust her bloom was hurled,
Still rich in beauty and grace, but not in power!
Then liberty seemed alone to live, for a while,
In Rome's imperial smile,
Sweetening its pride, as though
Stern crags by some tumultuous sea should feel
Their jagged bleakness bathed in a rosy glow.
Then came libidinous times that saw men kneel
Before base rulers wallowing in lust,
To-day on luxury gorged, with bloated face
Brow-bound in festal flowers, to-morrow thrust
As strangled corpses from that purple place
They soiled with splendors of disgrace!
Then liberty vanished wholly, and no more
Did palaces or lowlier homes less fair
Reveal her sculptural face and starry eyes,
Her timorous yet archangelic air.
But now with sinewy and sharp-taloned hand,
Fierce superstition, clutching at Europe's throat,
Dragged her to shadowy durance, and she lay

Loaded with fetters, far from liberal day,
In bigotry's dungeons, deep, remote,
While myriad martyrs died within her land
By stake and gibbet and rack; for the sweet sway
Of Christ, who had come to save and not to slay,
Was turned a bloody despotism, a band
Of tigerish dogmas that lurked, leapt and smote,
Howling inquisitorial howls above their prey!

VIII.

So prospering, wrong abode;
But her dark reign was broken at times with light,
For the star of Milton owed
Its lonely splendor to the age's night,
And later with clear silvery vigor glowed
The fire of Locke's pure wisdom, calmly bright;
Or yet across the opaque heaven men saw go
The audacious meteor-spirit of Rousseau! . . .
But not on Eastern lands, when the hour was ripe,
Nay, not in Eastern air, when the night was done,
Rose liberty's beauteous reascendant sun!
Not Italy saw the dawn's fair damask stripe,
Nor yet the glory of that large dazzling glance
Had fallen upon pale hunger-maddened France.
America, thou alone wert chosen on earth
Out of all nations joyously to hold

That dewy sunrise, of so noble a gold,
Which bathed thy meadowy slopes in lavish beams,
And made circuitous pomp of thy proud streams,
And turned thy solemn ocean to one scintillant mirth!

IX.

But this glad generous glory did not fall
On ivied abbey or palatial stair,
On statued gallery or superb parterre,
On turreted castle or manorial hall;
It fell on simple cottages, rude and spare;
It fell on laboring lives low-bowed with care;
It fell where drave the rigorous plough and where
The unrusted hay-fork glittered by the granary-wall.
A few brave spirits that long have passed away,
A few brave spirits, on that far April day,
Fought, lost, and losing still most royally won.
For from that hour, which was a world's dismay,
From that long-vanished hour's brief desperate fray,
Freedom's pure beautiful lips could smile and say:
"O men of all lands, look! I have had my Lexington!"
Preluded thus, how memorably rose
That bitter struggle of wrongers against wronged,
And with what peerless prominence largely glows
Out from the obscurer mass of these and those,
That soul in which all godlier gifts belonged!

How loftily in this one life were seen
Simplicity, self-denial, truth austere,
While, like the enwreathing vine about the oak,
In delicate breeding and suave ease of mien,
In all fine courteous affability, spoke
The gallantry of an old-world cavalier!
What stoic patience nerved his lightest breath
In that long arduous fight's ordeal severe,
And on the indomitable breadth and height
Of his supernal virtue, towering white,
How sightless calumny dashed itself to death!
Sire of our dear Republic, and yet son,
True gentleman, blameless ruler, matchless man,
Our model and type, our first American, —
Nay, all of lordlier meaning that no words have won
Till baffled eulogy pauses and says simply — Washington!

X.

But others, honored warriors, men of steel,
Stood round him, ready and eager in devotion,
Strong hewers of that majestic commonweal
Wrought with great blows in battle's hot commotion.
Men following him, their stainless leader, gladly;
Men prompt to seize and use all valued chances;
Men cunning and quick in feints, retreats, advances,
And yet, when the hour to fight came, fighting madly!

Eternal gratitude unto these, who wrested
Our future fate from tyranny, lion-hearted!
Eternal gratitude! since for us they breasted
Red war's tempestuous worst in days departed!
With fadeless reverence be their names invested,
And clothed with love as with a sheltering raiment,
And may the exalted work they grandly started
Render their memory its own sacred payment!
Bluff Putnam, fresh from the plough, a brawny yeoman;
Greene, lover of discipline, yet just, impartial;
Proud Schuyler, courtliest friend and bitter foeman;
Lee, faulty and yet fine-toned, with bearing martial;
The valorous Lafayette, the dashing Marion;
Tough Ethan Allen, with his grandiose phrases;
Montgomery, name beloved by glory's clarion;
Stark; Morgan; Wayne — oh, let the bounteous praises
Of these whose patient bravery broke our fetters,
Of these who won the immortal aim they sought for,
Of these, our stanch progenitors and our betters,
Gleam out, above the applausive land they fought for,
From history's brazen shaft in sculptured letters!

XI.

Mighty Republic, intensely
To these men, by rich obligations,
Thy years adolescent thou owest,

Since only through these men thou glowest
To-day this divine star of nations!
And yet how thy future immensely
Foretokens new splendors unbounded!
Its deep, though an ocean not sounded
That infinite mystery urges
With movements of vast variations,
Will yet, on allegiant surges,
In billowy vassalage, bear thee
Great gifts for thy service and pleasure,
That thou, if God prosper and spare thee,
Shalt regally welcome and treasure!

XII.

For lo, thou standest where the dolorous thunder
    Of ruining wrong sweeps backward with the night,
Where deadly mists of ignorance, broken asunder,
    Divide round wisdom's incontaminate height.
Thou seest, with brows of beautiful defiance
    And eyes whose arrowy lightnings cleave or scorch,
The fearless and imperial shape of Science
    Appall the darkness with her glorious torch!
Thou seest some outrage her bold foot is spurning
    Bring with its fall some hideous ill to light,
As, at some ponderous boulder's overturning,
    Some venomous length may coil itself to smite.

Thou seest how all the crimes of perished ages,
  Wrought in Christ's memory, her fine soul disdains;
All terrible engines of old priestly rages,
  Fierce torturing racks and blood-encrusted chains;
Crusades and leagues and all the old dead defences
  Of arrogant creeds now crumbling to decay,
From that wild massacre of the Albigenses
  To the dark anguish of Bartholomew's day.
Thou seest and meetest her in proud alliance,
  One old with knowledge, one in halcyon youth,
One our Republic, one invincible Science,
  Arch-foe and fierce Apollyon to untruth.
And down the shadowy future's gleaming spaces,
  Two stately goddesses, may you journey then,
Alike yet differing, as two sister Graces,
  Knowledge and Freedom visible among men.
So may your influence turn the louder quarrels,
  Or slumberous enmities of class and clime,
To lovelier manners and more lofty morals,
  And virtues blossoming with the touch of time!
Till slowly all humanity through the ample
  Planet of its abiding feels at length,
Below your bright supremity of example,
  Its genius broaden into kinglier strength.
And then, obedient to divine indenture,
  Our destiny shall roll on, we dream not how,

Toward some Hesperian bourne where peradventure
    The exultant souls of poets wait it now!
And on the unmastered passions, heart-enslaving,
    Shall intellect throne herself for royal sway,
And grosser lusts and all low sensual craving
    From the white spirit of man shall drop away.
And charity's mother-life, with joy seraphic,
    Shall nourish upon its bosom countless loves,
And commerce, freed from tyrannies of base traffic,
    Shall send her strong ships forth, like carrier-doves.
And holier laws of health shall bring their sequel
    Of shining bodily beauty, grace and might;
And opposite to the man, yet nobly equal,
    The woman shall achieve her loftiest right.
And then from perfect marriages whose calm sweetness
    No glimmer of sorrow mars, no dream of strife,
Some perfect race being born, whose rich completeness
    O'ershadows utterly all precedent life,
For this, perchance, toward some last goal translated,
    Which life and immortality meet to share,
In grand apocalypse, at the moment fated,
    The mystery of all time shall be laid bare!

THE SINGING OF LUIGI.

VENICE, A.D. 1430.

FOR Luigi, Duke Foscari's high-born page,
    The great court-ladies burned with tender rage.

But he, dark-clad, a shape of perfect mould,
With hair bushed outward, like a mist of gold,

Passed on, indifferent to their dainty grace,
Lowering unmoved his pale poetic face.

Yet sometimes, when the luminous lagoons
Drowsed in the mild Venetian afternoons,

The ducal gondola, brocaded fair,
Went slipping from the white palatial stair,

And ringed with dames and nobles, pensive, mute,
Young star-eyed Luigi leaned upon his lute.

Then some one, as the rich bark stole along,
Would plead with this grave minstrel for a song.

THE SINGING OF LUIGI.

And he, from reverie lured by such request,
Would muse a moment ere he acquiesced.

Then soon his voice would soar with golden ease
Above imperial porch and sculptured frieze.

From many a lattice eager heads would peer;
The oars were stayed by many a gondolier.

To hark the enchanting strains of this rare boy,
Half silver-streeted Venice paused with joy.

Through every tone sped passion's vibrant fire;
In each bold cadence throbbed ideal desire.

Here pangs of grief that words had found too strong,
Failing in words, failed sweetlier still in song;

Despair transcending speech here sought in vain
The melody to immortalize its pain;

And thus from passion, grief, desire, despair,
A wondrous eloquence floated into air,

So wild, so keen, so plaintive, so profound,
'Twas anguish, yearning, love, though still 'twas sound! . . .

For Luigi long had felt his bosom glow
Toward Lisa Nani, named the Maid of Snow.

She, born from lineage of princely note,
With amber tresses and pure swan-like throat,

Wandered her palace on Giudecca's tide,
Careless of suitors in her lonely pride.

But when the songs of Luigi met her ear,
Listening as one deep-stirred by secret fear,

Behind the tapestries that hid her form
The cold maid trembled and her cheek grew warm.

And now, one evening, it befell at last,
That while the boat of Luigi glided past,

And while he made, with all accustomed zeal,
His lovely spirituality of appeal,

Quick from the armorial window of her bower
Lisa bent down and cast to him a flower . . .

That night, bewildered by the bliss he felt,
Within a lordly chamber Luigi knelt.

THE SINGING OF LUIGI.

The two chaste hands that Lisa let him take
Fluttered like lilies on a windy lake.

The statue breathed; no longer calm and proud,
The goddess had descended from her cloud!

And kneeling thus, half doubtful if he dreamed,
To Luigi, in that sacred tryst, it seemed

That Fortune from her weird wheel sent the sound
Of marvellous music while she whirled it round!

.   .   .   .

Tedious the brief betrothal proved for both,
Ere the glad lovers took their marriage-oath.

With twenty gondolas for escort gay,
To San Giovanni's church they sailed away.

Here, in the holy gloom about them shed,
With stately ceremonial they were wed.

And when the bridal band, to mirth released,
Fared lightly homeward for the nuptial-feast,

A full moon, wrapt with wan haze like a robe,
Poised in the early dusk her ghostly globe.

And then to Luigi, seated near his bride,
Looking as one whom joy has deified,

The courtiers called, in many a merry row:
"Sing for us, Luigi, — sing, *carissimo!*"

And from vague balconies or casements high,
A watchful multitude caught up the cry,

Re-echoing it, in manner loud or low,
"Sing for us, Luigi, — sing, *carissimo!*"

Then Luigi, as the flattering summons rang,
Looked in the face of his dear bride, and sang.

Once more upon the city, like a thrall,
Delicious expectation seemed to fall.

The breeze of night seemed lingering in the sky;
Slower the wide canal seemed loitering by.

Below each bank in still more sombre mood
Its dull reduplication seemed to brood. . . .

So Luigi sang, and all the twilight dim
As though in reverent heed encompassed him.

But while his fine clear singing heavenward went,
In many a mind it woke bewilderment.

Here throve the old brilliant art, unhurt by change,
The delicate energy, the ample range,

The unstudied skill, the facile rise and fall,
The power, the euphony, the freshness — all!

And yet what nameless magic had dispelled
The inspiring soul these harmonies once held?

Where was the beautiful entreaty flung
At tyrant fate from the deep heart it wrung?

Where the choice genius that made song expand
With agony, with rebellion, with demand? . . .

From lip to lip the murmured comment flew;
At melancholy speed the amazement grew.

Then, like a skyward bird that droops its wing,
Luigi's ascendant voice forbore to sing.

The goal was reached; the attempted height was gained;
Struggle had vanquished; effort had attained.

All storms of suffering that once filled his breast
Had yielded to serenity of rest.

Sharp was the misery, in that former time,
Which made his piercing threnody sublime.

Tumultuous longing, fervid sense of wrong,
Had shaped the angelic pathos of the song.

And now its piteous ardor, its fond strife,
Ceased when the woe ceased that had lent them life! . . .

In Luigi's heart a furtive whisper said:
"The singer yet lives on, — the song is dead!"

Silent he sat, and gazed in Lisa's eyes,
Where sympathy was blended with surprise,

And where the unshed tears that obscured her sight
Had filmed their shadowy blue with wistful light.

Then soft she gave the answer love should give:
"Let the song die, if still the singer live!"

. . . .

Again the bridal band, to mirth released,
Fared lightly homeward for the nuptial-feast.

And this bright wedding, as years onward went,
Proved the sweet prelude of untold content.

But from that hour till his last hour was o'er,
Luigi, the lord of Lisa, sang no more!

THE RIVERS.

THOSE powers of the air that silent vigil keep,
    Roaming the long dim-galleried halls of sleep,
Bore me on their mysterious wings, one night,
Where pale voluminous vapors, huge of height,
Wrapt with solemnity no eye could pierce,
A dialogue of deep voices, proud and fierce.

THE NILE.

In Africa's midmost reaches, dumb and torrid,
    Where virgin lakes their opulent crystal spread,
By wastes of tangled foliage rankly florid,
Of old I raised to the sun my shining forehead,
    From cavernous earthy glooms that genii tread.
Here since primeval periods I have sundered
Hot banks that brute ferocity roamed and plundered,
Speeding, where turmoils of white cataract thundered,
    Toward lands my rich benignities have fed.

To these I have brought all nutritive existence,
  Alluvial benediction, priceless cheer;
Against aridity, patient in resistance,
My current, with unconquerable persistence,
  Has fought through many a prehistoric year.
The light, the life, the spirit of my dominion,
Alike I have lured the wild stork's wearied pinion,
Or in monotonous deserts Abyssinian
  The yellow ensanguined lions that prowled near.

But journeying southward in strong exultation,
  I attained that realm whose majesties are flown,
Egypt, with calm imperial sequestration
Uttering the genius of a mighty nation,
  Gathering her massive grandeurs near my own.
Built by laborious droves of captives lowly,
I watched her dull magnificence greaten slowly
To shapes of grim sarcophagi looming holy,
  Or grave miraculous palaces of stone.

I flowed by towering cities that have shaded
  My stream remotelier than all record saith,
With walls where hieroglyphs clung interbraided,
And avenues of tall sphinxes colonnaded
  Against the rainless heaven, serene of breath.
With temples reared by sovereignties tyrannic,

Gray mausoleums and monoliths titanic,
Frighting, in their tranquillity talismanic,
   Oblivion from the retinue of death!

I saw vast gods, for centuries unmolested,
   With fluted beards and bestial forms below;
Quaint cornices where the sacred sparrow nested;
Dense bands of ponderous pillars, lotus-crested,
   Thick-scrolled with many a weird intaglio;
Entablatures that showered among my sedges
The blood of quivering victims from their edges,
And those bold pyramids whose colossal wedges
   Not even an earthquake's arm could overthrow!

If fame might beam undimmed on history's pages,
   Thus Karnak, Thebes, Alexandria, Memphis would!
What dynasties that reached through shadowy ages!
What learning among papyri of old sages!
   What warriors battling for the civil good!
Yet in obscurity whence no hand releases,
How is that power and splendor fallen to pieces
Of lofty Ptolemies, lovely Berenices!
   Where is Cleopatra, star of womanhood?

Mute are the bacchanal feasts that filled my valleys
   With storms of dulcimers and with mirthful din;

Dead are my blossoming citrons, my palm-alleys;
Lost are the pomps of my luxurious galleys,
   With Nubian oarsmen clad in panther-skin.
Fled are the beauteous herds for Isis fatted;
In sandy burial or with moist weeds matted
Lie ruinous frieze or tumbled caryatid,
   Once reared to Osiris and his awful kin!

Propylons, grottos, hypogeums, medallions,
   The marvel of all has vanished as it rose;
Dusk armies glimmering in ornate battalions,
Monarchs who blazed with gems while sinewy stallions
   Drew them in radiant cars to meet their foes —
All, all have passed, and in their desolate places
The ironic present my domain disgraces;
Yet, ah! what land in rivalling wonder traces
   Memories like these of my dead Pharaohs!

THE EUPHRATES.

CEASE, impious boaster, with loud murmur lifted,
   To rank your perished affluence as divine,
And vaunt the expanses of your stream as gifted
   With lordlier reminiscences than mine!

For me, from Caucasus through bleak passes wending,
    Gorgeous Assyria's rarest charms were shown,
In all their warm exuberance far transcending
    Your stern monotonies of sepulchral stone.

I made no advent, whether speedy or gentle,
    Through blanks of landscape that all greeneries miss,
Journeying like you where torpors monumental
    Had girt you in one austere necropolis.
For me long prosperous decades brought their sequel,
    That stateliest city born beneath the sun!
How could your bulks of colorless granite equal
    The dazzling eminences of Babylon?

There Asshur, first of deities, reigned supernal,
    With shrines whose bright enormity overbrowed
The smoke of reverent sacrifice diurnal,
    Where the mitred priests in snowy raiments bowed.
There luscious fruitages poured copious measures;
    There gifts were stored from tributary states;
There camels, tottering under loads of treasures,
    Trooped with swart conquerors through the brazen gates.

To shawms and harps my revelling kings quaffed wassail,
    Between the august winged bulls, grotesque, severe,

Where the rainbow-hued pavilions rose colossal
    O'er high aerial gardens, tier on tier.
And night, made scintillant with its tossing torches,
    On silver and golden idols loved to shine,
On eunuchs lolling among the marble porches,
    On roses wreathen above Damascus wine.

Like locust-clouds our multitudinous forces
    Have swept with ravage along a thousand ways;
Like meteors our swift white Nisæan horses
    Have flashed with iron chariots through mad frays.
We smote our enemies, all who dared assail us,
    With javelins that no prowess of man out-thrust;
Sargon, Sennacherib, or Sardanapalus,
    Alike we have levelled kingdoms to the dust!

How regally since old Nimrod have our races
    Of stolid sovereigns waged their war-like harms,
With plumed tiaras above black-bearded faces
    And bracelets glittering on bare tawny arms!
How deep our cavalries ploughed slaughterous channels
    Through shuddering hosts that heard the keen bolts hiss!
How gloriously endures among our annals
    The martial dominance of Semiramis!

To Baal or Merodach ceaseless praise was tendered,
   Or Ashtaroth, sceptred with unearthly grace,
But haughtily fumed the frankincense we rendered
   To Ishtar, terrible goddess of the chase.
For breaking our voluptuous Asian languor,
   We rode as perilous pastime, without fear,
Where many a lion in his deadly anger
   Roared challenge to the invulnerable spear!

Nor paths of victory we alone have followed,
   But seers were ours, unravelling like a skein
The brilliant secrets of those heavens that hollowed
   Their dome above the immense Chaldean plain.
Here, though its fated edifice has been smitten,
   We watch our immortality throne her claim;
In stars our luminous epitaph is written;
   Eternity is custodian of our fame!

THE RHINE.

NAY, chant no more from burning climes
Your sensuous and fantastic rhymes,
In praise of those barbaric times
   Filled thick with rancorous legions.

How may such heathen deeds contrast,
Though once they have set the world aghast,
With that imperishable past
   Hallowing my winsome regions?

What Christly influence wraps my stream
With delicate sanctity supreme,
Like slumberous mists that brood and gleam
   When summer dawns are breathless!
What songs my haunted bosom sings
Of reverend legendary things,
In soft mediæval murmurings,
   Melodiously deathless!

Cologne, with what sublime consent
Have faith and poesy interblent
In smooth harmonious minglement,
   To achieve thy sacred token!
Behold the intense embodied prayer,
Whose words of stone are uttering there
One silent *Credo* in sculpture, where
   The *Amen* is still unspoken!

Within my broad mellifluous tide
Inveterate souvenirs abide

Of saintly trust, of knightly pride,
  Going forth as dread invaders.
Continual visions crowd my banks
Of stalwart steeds with blazoned flanks,
That eastward bore in tireless ranks
  The old hardy-thewed Crusaders!

I saw wide monasteries crown
The crags that o'er my waters frown,
Where nuns with pensive eyes looked down,
  While evening dews fell moister;
Or where the tonsured monks would bow,
Obedient to their priestly vow,
Before Our Lady's aureoled brow,
  In many a lonesome cloister.

For me the fat bluff burgher quaffed
Brown ale when freed from toilful craft,
With many a gay jest, while he laughed,
  That kind remembrance harbors;
For me the Minnesingers made
Lyrics where halcyon fancies played,
Like variant sunbeams mixed with shade
  Below their grape-hung arbors.

The aromas of romantic lore
Yet linger round my sacred shore,

Where ghostly nixies combed of yore
   Blond locks that coiled and glistened;
Where cold swan-maidens glided white,
Where elves held carnival by night,
Where the lone Lorelei on the height
   Sang death to all who listened!

Ah, still gold-haired Gunhilda tells
The undying tale of Drachenfels;
Through Zündorf still, by darksome spells,
   The Wasserman spreads deep sadness;
In vale or thicket still I note
The erl-kings and the fairies float,
Or that fleet will-o'-the-wisp who smote
   The Kreutzberg monk with madness!

But dolorous deeds have stained me red
When feudal princes met and bled,
When troops of desperate peasants fled
   While baron-thieves marauded;
I saw dense fights round bastioned towers,
Meek maidens ravished from their bowers,
And insolent prelates mock the powers
   Their soldieries defrauded.

Yet spite of hours thus dimmed with woe,
This heaven above me smiles to know

That peerless among all kin I flow
    Beneath its blue pavilions.
Dead Chivalry's dearest worth was mine;
Unique, incomparable, I shine,
The old castle-skirted storied Rhine,
    Beloved by bordering millions!

THE AMAZON.

PAUSE in your resonant turmoil and patiently hearken
    To me while I sing,
Rivers, whose fame I eclipse as a tempest will darken
    The world with its wing.
Mine is the candid unmanacled liberty owning
    No mortal's light sway;
Kindred am I to all winds in their moving and moaning,
    And tameless as they.
One my circuitous roamings, my rhythmic pulsations,
    With stars where they roll;
Man cannot fathom the fire of those large inspirations
    That warm my great soul!
He that would utter my name in its meaning stupendous,
    With all it enshrouds,
Must for the words that he uses take torrents tremendous,
    Take mountains and clouds.

Lo, I am lifted above insubstantial traditions,
      Nor heed while they pass;
Less to my forest-clad pride are a kingdom's transitions
      Than dewfalls on grass.
All the base multiform passion whose energy urges
      The heart of mankind,
Shelters among the brute creatures that wander my verges,
      Thick-leaved, lavish-vined.
Here in my leopards and serpents are fostered and hidden
      The crafts and the greeds
Wrought with coeval resemblance to longings forbidden
      That sway human deeds.
Yet as the adequate symbol of virtues resultant
      From aims that exalt,
Heaven at my summons will glass in these waters exultant
      Her uttermost vault.
Discords are mine that can drown all the trivial dissensions
      Of men far and near;
Euphonies float from my surge whose harmonious dimensions
      Even gods could not hear.
Go where superb white audacity tells its defiance
      In peaks robed with snows;

There shall you learn that infrangible bonds of alliance
    Have bound me to those.
Go where the pinnacled ice rims the ghastly north oceans
    Through months of keen night;
There, amid altitudes glacial and thunderlike motions,
    Live moods of my might.
Breaths of terrific simooms, making caravans tremble,
    Possess, while they fly,
Onslaught and turbulence, courage and speed, that resemble
    This power that is I!
Be it the vast winding cave, or the Alp lightnings blister,
    Or the cliff huge, austere,
Each in its grandeur profound I accept as my sister, —
    Yet scorn as my peer!
Whence, in my vigorous attainment, my visage resplendent,
    Till time shall have flown,
I, of all rivers terrestrial, am chief and transcendent,
    Elect and alone!

THE THAMES.

RING on, dissentient cries,
Whose boisterous echoes rise
And fill with acrimonious vaunts the unsympathetic
skies!
I neither praise nor blame
The lineage you proclaim;
Not mine the arbitrament that seals your glory or your
shame.

Perchance I too might sing
Of army and court and king,
Of proud pictorial episodes where swords and helmets
ring.
Perchance my voice might tell
What happy memories dwell
Where England's meadowy distances like music fall and
swell.

But rather would I find
In the onward march of mind
Strong right to achieve supremacy and rule above my
kind.

For me 't was given to know
Gross prejudice flung low,
And science levelling fable in victorious overthrow.

Philosophy's full beam
Has bathed my honored stream,
And guided men toward nobler moods than superstitious dream.
Here fact, crying out "I am,"
Stripped sophistry of sham;
Here throve the effulgent intellect of matchless Verulam.

Here temperate self-control
Calmed freedom's fiery soul,
Reversing her impetuous course toward wisdom's rugged goal;
Here reason's lips have wound
The clarion whose clear sound
Sent dogma whimpering from the prey its greedy fangs had found.

Tired out with guile, intrigue,
An irresistible league,
My people in fervid action showed their agonized fatigue.

Not with the crimson reek
Of scaffolds did they speak,
But through the broadening girth of limbs that made
their fetters weak.

Lo, now the shadow is fled
Whose blackness overspread
The starry undaunted eyes of truth and her seraphic
head;
Lo, progress, harshly wroth,
Frights bigotry like a moth
When brushed from out the broideries of some ancient
arras-cloth.

The mightier minds no more
Waste effort to explore
Infinity's ocean, breaking on an unconjectured shore.
They turn from the empty task
Of tearing her close mask
Off the Isis whose oracular mouth denies them what
they ask.

Their impulse aims, instead,
With equal steps to tread
The arduous jeopardy called life, where many a foot has
bled;

They heed the woful tone
Of crushed humanity's moan;
They leave the unknowable to dwell at peace with God, the unknown.

They hold as worthiest prayer
To assuage the long despair
That poverty's fell ubiquity makes drudging millions bear;
They search, by pity taught,
All the arsenals of thought
For weapons murderous to the wrongs that ignorance has wrought.

They see, like streaks of day
In heaven's far doubtful gray,
The auroral evidence of love, and hate's dark disarray.
They send toward purer things
Desires whose journeyings
Are larks that dare the unventured dusk with sweet adventurous wings.

Yet while by stubborn deeds
Their fresh unfaltering creeds
Have reached through hollow pomps of cant reality's vital needs,

Ah, where on the earth save here,
Co-operant in career,
Do all man's godliest attributes converge and persevere?

THE SEA.

HAVE peace, be still,
O frivolous throngs, that feed me, rill by rill!
Vex with contentious interludes no more
My sweeps of shore!

Enough to know
Your duty as ye subserviently flow;
Enough that ye were wrought to augment my waves,
Poor clamoring slaves!

Wedded to me
As limb to body or skin to flesh are ye,
And all your confluent lives, till this life die, —
Behold they are I!

A VENGEANCE.

FROM savage pass and rugged shore
　　The noise of angry hosts had fled;
The bitter battle raged no more.
Where fiery bolts had wrought their scars,
And where the dying and the dead
In many a woful heap were flung,
While night above the Ægean hung
Its melancholy maze of stars.

One boyish Greek, of princely line,
Lay splashed with blood and wounded sore;
His wan face in its anguish bore
That delicate symmetry divine
Carved by the old sculptors of his land.
A broken blade was in his hand,
Half slipping from the forceless hold
That once had swayed it long and well;
And round his form in tatters fell
The velvet raiment flowered with gold.

But while the calm night later grew,
He heard a stealthy and rustling sound,
Like one who trailed on laggard knee
A shattered shape along the ground.
And soon with sharp surprise he knew
That in the encircling gloom profound
A fierce Turk crawled by slow degrees
To where in helpless pain he lay.
Then, too, he witnessed with dismay
That from the prone Turk's rancorous eye
Flashed the barbaric lurid trace
Of hate's indomitable hell, —
Such hate as death alone could quell,
As death alone could satisfy.

Closer the loitering figure drew,
With naked bosom red from fight,
With ruthless fingers clutching tight
A dagger stained by murderous hue.
Till now, in one great lurch, he threw
His whole frame forward, aiming quick
A deadly inexorable blow,
That weakly faltering, missed its mark,
And left the assassin breathing thick,
Levelled by nerveless overthrow,
There near the Greek chief, in the dark.

Then he that saw the baffled crime,
Half careless of his life's release,
Since death must win him soon as prey,
Turned on his foe a smile sublime
With pity, and the stars of Greece
Beheld him smile, and only they.

All night the two lay side by side,
Each near to death, yet living each;
All night the grim Turk moaned and cried,
Beset with pangs of horrid thirst,
Save when his dagger crept to reach,
By wandering ineffectual way,
The prostrate Greek he yearned to slay,
And failure stung him till he cursed.

But when soft prophecies of morn
Had wrapt the sea in wistful white,
A band of men, with faces worn,
Clomb inland past a beetling height,
To find the young chief they adored,
Sought eagerly since fall of sun
And now in ghastly change restored . . .
One raised a torch of ruddy shine,
And kneeling by their leader, one
Set to his mouth a gourd of wine.

Then the young Greek, with wave of hand,
Showed the swart Pagan at his side,
So motioning to the gathered band
That none could choose but understand.

"Let this man drink!" he said, and died.

A MOOD OF CLEOPATRA.

"*Au temps de Cléopâtre . . . on eût fait venir six ou cinq esclaves, mâles ou femelles, et l'on aurait essayé le poison sur eux; on aurait fait ce que les médecins appellent une expérience* in anima vili. . . . *Une douzaine de misérables se seraient tordus comme des anguilles coupées en morceaux sur les beaux pavés de porphyre et les mosaïques étincelantes, devant la maîtresse . . . suivant de son regard velouté les dernières crispations de leur agonie.*"

THÉOPHILE GAUTIER.

CLEOPATRA, when the chilling fear
   Of ruin touched her soul at ease,
When turbid sounds, blown over seas,
Would speed on rumor's rapid path
From the hot lips of Roman wrath
Straight to her own Egyptian ear, —
Then, even at some grand feast of hers,
Would seem to feel the joy struck dumb
Of citherns, harps and dulcimers,
With rumbling prelude, harsh to hear,

Of that which must in time become
Disaster, slavery, Actium!

Then she, that mighty and mystic queen,
Round whom her vassals crawled in awe,
Whose lifted finger was a law,
Whose smile an edict, and whose frown
A darkness on the lands between
Arabian wave and Libyan dust,
Whose name, tyrannic and august,
From marbleful Syene's town
On wings of wonderment flew down
The old sacred Nile and serpentine
North to Canopus and the sea, —
Cleopatra, couched at feast, even she,
In lovely sovereignty supine,
Would quiver with a sudden sigh,
And one imperious hand would raise
That bade the revel's music die,
And made, along its mighty maze
Of columned galleries grandly high,
A silence as of death to come
On all the vast triclinium!

"If I must die," her thought would say,
"What way shall be the swiftest way?

What subtle drug shall give release
With slightest pain before it slay,
And make my conqueror find me here
As one who thrids in cavernous night
Some hypogeum's halls austere,
Expecting when his steps shall cease
Beside the uncrumbled cryptic peace
Of still sarcophagi, and when
He shall behold, with sharp delight,
With thrills of greed he shall behold,
The royal mummies lying rolled
In lordliest wealth against his sight,
Richly embalmed, these kings renowned,
In naphtha and bitumen bound:
But now he gains their bourne of sleep,
And sees their gilded coffers rise,
Stript of all wealth to clutch and keep,
Plundered and spoiled ere this by those
Who have dared in violative wise
To assault with strong and impious blows
The old awful slumbering Pharaohs.
Thus even shall he that finds me here
Find ruin of what I was alone,
The dumb bulk left, the life outflown,
Beyond all shadow of shame or fear,
Since Death can do whatso he please

With whoso he shall choose to strive,
But Roman hands, though quick to seize,
Can never manacle alive,
With wrist-gyve or with ankle-gyve,
The daughter of the Ptolemies!

"Wherefore, if I must die one day,
How fleetest shall this flesh get peace?
What way shall be the swiftest way?
What subtle drug shall give release
With slightest pain before it slay?"

Then would she clap her small swart hands,
And soon the obeisant slaves would bring
Rare cups and goblets, oddly wrought
With sculptured shapes in circling bands,
Or many a strange hieratic thing
Whereof these latter times and lands
Know either vaguely or know naught —
With Athor, Isis, one-armed Khem,
Snake, scarab, ibis, wingèd ball,
Quaint coptic anaglyph; and all
These vessels, to the brims of them,
With deadliest poisons had been fraught.

Then slowly, through the hall's great space,
Where, statued in weird hybrid gloom,
With black claws crost in cold repose,

The lofty basalt sphinxes loom, —
Between the pillars huge of base
That might bear heaven, if so they chose,
On bulging chapiters that enthrone
Colossal lotos-leaves of stone, —
Before the queen, with timorous pace,
With groundward brow and quivering limb,
With horror on each haggard face,
They come, the slaves that are to die
Beneath Cleopatra's critic eye,
And pleasure so her sovereign whim.

They dare not make one lightest moan,
While ranging in a dreadful file
Before their slayer's icy smile.
They dare alone to cower and shrink;
Alone they dare to obey, alone
To grasp their goblets and be dumb;
For tortures worse than death might come,
Did they rebel in prayer and groan.
Some sweat with anguish as they drink;
Some totter and have bristling hair;
Some choke their bitter sobs, and some
Roll eyeballs awful with despair!

Poisons are here of taste and hue
Differing, yet each of baleful might;

For here is hellebore, aconite,
Henbane, euphorbia; these, and more
Known only in the years of yore.

And all are drunken to the lees
By those poor minion lips accurst.
A fearful quiet falls at first
Over the doomed ones where they stand,
Till now they sink by sure degrees,
Form after stricken form, beneath
The smile so fathomlessly bland
Of the calm queen who hears and sees
Their anguish of the stiff crooked hand,
The writhen body and gnashing teeth,
The blackening tongues, the crimsoned eyes,
The foaming bloated lips, the cries
That up those monstrous galleries ring
In mad debauch of suffering!

Superb doth Queen Cleopatra sit,
The fragrant feast-flowers on her hair,
And o'er the shadowy waves of it,
Her crown imperially fair
For spikes of gold about the brows.
The delicate schenti that allows
Glimpses of her voluptuous shape,

Doth her firm bend of bosom drape,
And lightlier lies on her brown limbs
Than on some moonlit mountain's base
The gauziest vapor-wreath that swims.
From either side her languorous face
The fringy calisiris flows;
A gorget girds her olive throat,
Fantastic, beautiful to note,
Where clear-green chrysoberyl glows
Beside azedarach, in rows.

One marvellous arm supports her head,
With dull gold six times braceleted,
As backward on the empurpled case
Of her Greek couch she leans at rest.
Her deepening smile hath half confest
That one thing yet holds power to please
Her tired soul pleasure-surfeited.
One thing: this riot of death she sees,
This pomp of human pangs unblest,
This revel of ghastly agonies!

And so, while at her feet they writhe, —
While levelled of their torture sore
They grovel on the porphyry floor,
These slaves, whose life is almost less

In Egypt than to crush a gnat, —
Then (oh, strange change to wonder at!)
Cleopatra's smile turns bright and blithe,
Her eyelids lose their heaviness,
Her long deep eyes begin to shine,
And reaching one dark faultless hand
Where the gold festal goblets stand
Carved by Lysippus' rare finesse
In sculptures worthy hands divine,
For veriest joy her red mouth laughs,
As now with back-flung head she quaffs
The odorous white Mareotic wine!

THE GIRL AT THE CROSSING.

SHE was just sixteen, that night, as she stood
In her ragged dress and her rusty hood.

She had swept the crossing the same old way
You have seen the beggars do, any day,

With first a rush to the passer's side,
Then a dash ahead, and the broom well plied,

And then, as she gained the curb, you know,
The ancient professional moan of woe.

But now she is tired; the night grows late;
She leaves the crossing with laggard gait.

And as she passes the street lamp's glare,
You catch the sheen of her unkempt hair,

Falling to meet, with its tangled flow,
The two great weary black eyes below.

THE GIRL AT THE CROSSING.

She goes from haunts of the rich and sleek
To dull-lit regions of murk and reek;

And under a lamp that flickers frail,
In the sudden breath of the autumn gale,

Pausing she searches her dress, to drag
From its pocket a dingy twisted rag,—

Her pennies, earned through the long day, all
Lumped into this unsightly ball.

With a feeble smile she counts them o'er,
And is slipping them out of sight once more,

When a hand from the dimness, quick and bold,
Tears the rag from her careless hold.

She cries out sharply; a form shoots fleet,
Yards beyond, through the vague void street.

. . . .

She stands in the doorway; she does not stir;
While her drunken father scowls at her.

He has wondered long that she still should stay,
For he craved her earnings to drink away.

With trembling voice, in her words uncouth,
She tells him simply the simple truth.

He lifts his hand, while his dull eyes glow,
And strikes her down with a brutal blow!

. . . .

You may see her now, any night that's fair,
In a certain street, by a certain square. . . .

See her well, if you wait for a little while,
In her silken dress, with her brazen smile! . . .

IDEALS.

O SCIENCE, whose footsteps wander,
   Audacious and unafraid,
Where the mysteries that men ponder
   Lie folded in awful shade,
Though you bring us, with calm defiance,
   Dear gifts from the bournes you wing,
There is yet, O undaunted Science,
   One gift that you do not bring!

Shall you conquer the last restriction
   That conceals it from you now,
And come back with its benediction
   Like an aureole on your brow?
Shall you fly to us, roamer daring,
   Past barriers of time and space,
And return from your mission bearing
   The light of God on your face?

We know not, but still can treasure,
    In the yearning of our suspense,
Consolation we may not measure
    By the certitudes of sense;
For life, as we long and question,
    Seems to bear, while it hurries by,
Through undertones of suggestion,
    Immortality's deep reply!

To ears that await its token
    Perpetually it strays
Indeterminate, fitful, broken
    By the discords of our days!
It pierces the grim disasters
    Of clamorous human hate,
And its influence overmasters
    All the ironies of fate!

The icy laugh of the scorner
    Cannot strike its echoes mute;
It cleaves the moan of the mourner
    Like a clear æolian lute.
At its tone less keen and savage
    Grows the anguish of farewell tears,
And its melody haunts the ravage
    Of the desecrating years!

IDEALS.

Philosophy builds, and spares not
   Her firm laborious power;
But her lordly edifice wears not
   Its last aerial tower,
For the quarries of reason fail her
   Ere the structure's perfect scope,
And the stone that would now avail her
   Must be hewn from heights of hope!

But Art, at her noblest glory,
   Can seem, to her lovers fond,
As divinely admonitory
   Of infinitudes beyond.
She can beam upon earth's abasement
   Like splendor flung down sublime
Through a vague yet exalted casement
   From eternity into time!

On the canvas of some great painter
   We may trace, in its varied flame,
Now leaping aloft, now fainter,
   As the mood uplifts the aim,
That impulse by whose rare presence
   His venturing brush has drawn
Its hues from the efflorescence
   Of a far Elysian dawn!

SONG AND STORY.

An impassioned watcher gazes
    Where the faultless curves combine
That sculpture's mightier phases
    Imperially enshrine,
And feels that by strange election
    The artificer's genius wrought
From the marble a pale perfection
    That is paramount over thought!

So in music entranced we wonder,
    If its charm the spirit seeks,
When with mellow voluminous thunder
    A sovereign maestro speaks,
Till it seems that by ghostly aidance
    Upraised above lesser throngs,
He has caught from the stars their cadence
    And woven the winds into songs!

More than all, if the stately brilliance
    Of a poet's rapture rise,
Like a fountain whose full resilience
    Is lovely against clear skies,
We are thrilled with a dream unbounded
    Of deeps by no vision scanned,
That conjecture has never sounded
    And conception has never spanned!

So the harvest that knowledge misses
   Intuition seems to reap;
One pauses before the abysses
   That one will delight to leap.
One balks the ruminant sages,
   And one bids the world aspire,
While the slow processional ages
   Irreversibly retire!

THE DOUBTER.

A stretch of low shore, on which the ocean breaks with large noisy waves. A man and woman stand here. They clasp each other's hands. Both faces are filled with agony. The man speaks.

LOVE, your hair loosens, the winds have their will with it,
    Half its warm affluent amber dishevelling;
Now they uplift it and now they lie still with it,
    Salt from the sea on whose deeps they are revelling.
Stand with me, sweet, while the wave topples thunderous,
    While the dim gull dares the morning's immensity,
O'er us the sky's blue infinitude, under us
    Reaches of swart shore and rocks in dark density.

Here we clasp hands with pale faces and pleasureless,
    We with no heart for the light lapsing glorious
On till it dies among distances measureless,
    On till it bathes among billows uproarious.

Earth in her absolute happiness heeds us not,
    Turned like some haughty implacable heart from us;
Proud with supreme pride, she knows us not, needs us
    not,
    Laughs and is lovely aloof and apart from us.

Grief, like the scriptural angel imperial,
    Points with stern finger the path for our feet to tread;
Seen far away, rosy-robed and ethereal,
    Love treads with weeping the ways we found sweet
    to tread.
Oh the lost future, the doom dictatorial,
    Dark with its curse of unchangeable severance!
Ah, the fair past, the flown moments memorial,
    Shrine where the sad thought pays passionate rev-
    erence!

Fleetly indeed fades the joy life may hold for us,
    Brief is our breath ere the end shall annihilate.
How can we guess what the future may hold for us,
    Draped with a darkness no vision may violate?
Starless, opaque, irresponsive, inscrutable,
    Who hath had eyes that might pierce the hard
    mystery?
Who of the prophets, the many, the mutable,
    Crowding with creeds the long highways of history.

This we have learned after questioning querulous,
　This we have learned after longing importunate:
Life, whether painful or easeful or perilous,
　Closes in death, whether woful or fortunate.
Not though the body and spirit both bleed for it,
　More shall we learn while the centuries glide from us;
Not though in awful ineffable need for it,
　Praying we fling the last fragment of pride from us!

Wherefore I say if a man hath loved urgently,
　Given all his heart for a woman's dear pleasurement,
(Just as a wave with white worship insurgently
　Rushes to mantle some crag's mighty measurement,)
How shall he tamely see fate in her dominance
　Tear from his keeping what kings could not buy from it?
See hope drop down, as in flame-shrouded prominence
　Drops the doomed ship when the frighted throngs fly from it?

You that are fair as a flower-stem is frangible,
　Chaster than dawns with no shadow of night in them,
Filled with all graces intense though intangible,
　Having the eyes with the deep dreamy light in them!
More do I need you, my pure-browed, my beautiful,
　Than the star needs the blue fathoms it burns within,

More than the grove its bird-vassalage dutiful,
   Or the mossed mill-wheel the stream that it turns within!

All things earth shows me, through years yet unborn for me,
   Lovely or lordly, in lineaments numberless,
Though they still wear the old charm they have worn for me,
   Yet shall wake yearning, unquenchable, slumberless.
Opulent pastures, or sun-fall's cloud-palaces
   Clear purple mountains or meadowlands flowerful,
Riot of roses or chaste lily-chalices,
   Each will bear sign of you, sacred and powerful.

Never an evening shall shape in the west of it
   Any frail crescent's new silver fragility,
Never a sea-wave shall wreathe on the crest of it
   Any full moonbeam's quick pale instability,
But, O my sweet, in the delicate thrall of these,
   Luring my spirit's allegiance and loyalty,
Linked by mysterious kinship to all of these,
   You shall still reign with unwavering royalty!

Ah, could I trust that these farewells for each of us
   Meant at the end but a fleet earthly vanishment,

That an eternal delight were in reach of us,
  Having flung down our dull burdens of banishment,
Then, though time smote me with savage hostilities,
  How I would stand hardy-fronted and towerlike!
Then, with a smile at all fate's possibilities,
  How I would wear my worst agony flowerlike! . . .

Still, O believers, if Christ could come down to you,
  Come from the cross where they nailed him, disdaining him,
Come bloody-browed from the terrible crown to you,
  Come with the insolent spear-wound yet staining him,
Half would desert his meek godhead denyingly,
  Spurned like the corpse by the conqueror's chariot,
Half would forsake him, as lightly, as lyingly,
  As the low soul of his own dead Iscariot!

Seen as an image illusive and vapory,
  Clad by the ages with blurring obscurity,
Reared statuesque o'er some altar's dark drapery,
  Love ye to praise your white Christ in his purity!
This is not he that wrought bounty from slenderness,
  Fed the large glad throng, while greater and lesser eat;
This is not he that with voice full of tenderness
  Called unto Peter at morn by Gennesaret!

This is no god that if raimented meagrely
    Yet with meek love like a raiment enfolding him,
They that now worship would turn upon eagerly,
    Turn with fond hearts that leapt high at beholding him.
Nay, they would let the rough rains work their worst on him,
    Let the snows freeze him, the mountain pass swallow him,
Leave the hot hate of the lightning to burst on him,
    Ere they would dare to rise up and to follow him!

Ah, were he stripped of the riches they gird him with,
    Few then would serve him in silent humility,
Changed from the old haughty gods they would herd him with,
    Loving heaped altars and pompous docility!
Oh, he is well, and his worship might never end
    While upon rich easy cushions they kneel to him,
Daintily godlike, conveniently reverend,
    Where the bland Pharisee legions appeal to him!

Say that the north wind the tender grass nourishes,
    Say that youth's hues are of all things the lividest,
Say of the rose that on frost-blight she flourishes,
    Say of the star that by noon she is vividest,

Say that all lives wear a touch of nobility,
  Say that the oak may not crush the anemone,
But call not this god of mere church-gentility
  Him that sweat blood in the glooms of Gethsemane!

   .   .   .   .

Look, the free sea, how it leaps on its sands to us,
  Strong with a strength that no woes may emaciate,
Waving afar its pale splendors of hands to us,
  Laughing with lips that no laughter may satiate.
Watch how the long surge goes wandering seeker-like,
  Reared of this sea, the old arrogant leveller;
Mark how the day seems to drink of it beaker-like,
  Drink and be glad, as an infinite reveller.

Beautiful wild-throated sea, you are pitiless,
  Proud in the power that we watch who are powerless,
Glad, though all earth should lie plundered and citiless,
  So you still break on your bleak shores and flower-
    less.
Sea, being free, being glad from the birth of you,
  How shall we make our supreme despair known to you,
Hearing the old immemorial mirth of you,
  Though in our greatness of anguish we moan to you?

Careless that sorrow should master and capture us,
  Roll your broad luminous waters resiliently;

Ah, for one tithe of the liberty rapturous
    Born in their amplitudes, arching so brilliantly!
Here by the sand where your billow breaks thunderful,
    Fair as when first the old mighty Greek sang of it,
We, by your stately delights and your wonderful,
    Take a last parting, with sobs at the pang of it!

CYNICISM.

FROM those who seize in sensual haste
    Life's best of fruitage, day by day,
Who eat with greed, revile the taste,
    Then cast the empty rind away;

From those who crave the moment's ease
    To miss the lifetime's larger cheer,
How false, how tame, from such as these,
    How slight of worth, the ironic sneer!

Off grave philosophy they steal
    The classic robe her stature vaunts,
Dress her anew and praise with zeal
    The bells and motley that she flaunts.

They carp at wisdom's gathered lore;
    They call her humblest maxims vain;
Disdaining dogma, they ignore
    The dogmas of their own disdain.

CYNICISM.

Ah, fatuous idlers, if ye will,
   Your lamps of banquet glitter bright,
But over them burn lovelier still
   The pale pavilions of the night!

Go, seek the man whose eyes have traced
   Experience to her utmost ends,
Whose long vicissitudes have faced
   Love's treachery and the loss of friends;

Whose years have tested, while they fled,
   How wrong may thrive with right low-flung;
Whose tears have dropped upon his dead,
   Hot from the anguish whence they sprung;

The man whom life has racked and worn,
   Yet mingled blessings with its blows —
Pierced by the poignance of its thorn,
   Yet given the richness of its rose;

The man of temperate mind and tongue,
   Who fairly met all change and chance,
Nor soothed caprice with pleasures wrung
   From unconsenting circumstance!

Go, seek this man, though cares enslave
   The last slow term of his career,
And ask him if he dares to waive
   The mighty problem with a sneer!

Or if, through hours of toil and ache,
   Has fluttered no mysterious breath,
Faint as a dream, yet strong to shake
   The bastions of the gates of death!

PORTENT.

I MUSE and read, from day to day,
  Of human thought's far-widening sway.
Its gradual exodus I note
From shadowy periods remote.

I see false faiths in ruin lie,
Whose thronging towers once cleft the sky.
I mark, amid the past's renown,
Colossal bigotries flung down!

And yet from history's feeblest youth
I watch in joy how deathless truth
Has striven to make, with stoic breast,
Her immortality manifest!

And now, since they that love her strive
To strip the last barbaric gyve
Off limbs that such rude furrows mar,—
A century's pain in every scar,—

At length from her glad lips may fall
Some holy oracle to appall;
Some priceless utterance that shall cause
A world to tremble with applause! . . .

Moments are mine when heaven's blue scope
Seems throbbing with mysterious hope,
And earth's great circuit seems no less
Thrilled by miraculous presages!

I seem to hear, on each new breeze,
Vague yet stupendous prophecies . . .
Deep awe possesses me . . . I feel
Stanch reason impotently reel. . . .

Where Science flies, with robes that shine,
Afar on embassies divine,
Dare we to dream her foot will press
Eternity's unknowableness?

Dare we to dream her hand will lay
Finality as bare as day,
And bring, for all dark doubts that brood,
Some lovely and mighty certitude?

Ah, who shall say? . . . The immense age waits;
Veiled are the faces of the fates;
While all things bode, in dread portent,
Some luminous and sublime event!

YESTERDAY.

WE are met, with tearless eyes,
    With variant sounds of sighs,
With souls that many memories fondly sway,
    We are met, we two alone,
    Where long winds move and moan,
We are met to make a grave for Yesterday.

    See on his piteous face
    The inalienable trace
Of morning and of youth's impetuous thrill;
    And wreathen amid his hair
    The ruin of roses there,
And amaranths where the dim dews linger still!

    Let his low grave lie deep
    For that sepulchral sleep
In glooms where blind oblivion loves to grope!
    Deep as our piercing care,
    And hollow as our despair,
And dark as the smouldering torches of our hope!

    About his rigid shape
    What drapery shall we drape
Against the unholy hands decay would reach?
    Let it be woven and wrought
    Of many a mournful thought,
Yet white as the faith once plighted each to each!

    What requiem shall we raise,
    Loveliest of Yesterdays,
Above the abasement of your brows divine?
    What coronal of sweet sound,
    In heavenly ways profound,
Shall music with aerial fingers twine?

    Let her take sobs of waves
    In void reverberant caves
Where the great sea's elegiac passion stirs;
    Let her take gales that go
    With dreary adagio
Through lonely leafage of funereal firs!

    Let her take doleful cries
    Of ominous birds in skies
That vaporous autumn twilights leave forlorn,
    Or chimes of chill cascades
    That plash through mountain-glades
From livid glaciers in the wintry morn!

Let her blend strains with these,
Heard through the Italian trees,
Through olive and ilex when the moon floats pale;
Strains rapturous and yet mild, —
That glory of grief, that wild
Melodious anguish named the nightingale!

O music, mix in one,
With eloquent unison,
All sorrowing chords that Nature's lyre can make,
Till your voluminous dirge
May echo and swell and surge,
And speak for the breaking hearts that mutely break!

What lavish flowers and leaves,
Exequial crowns or sheaves,
On his austere tranquillity may we strew?
Pale violets dead for years,
Bathed by dead lovers' tears,
With pathos lingering in their wistful blue!

Chaplets that brides have worn
When tyrannous war has torn
Young heart from quivering heart, with tortures keen;
Warm passion-flowers that show
Gethsemane in their glow,
And all the agony of the Nazarene!

Dusk myrtles that have grown
Round statues overthrown,
Pitying the crumbled grandeurs where they creep;
Poppies that softly bring
Opiates for suffering, —
Red vassals in the shadowy courts of sleep!

Ivy that wraps its bowers
Round gray disconsolate towers,
Where sombre tapestries wave in dusty state;
Grasses that lean and drip
O'er slumberous pools where slip
The stealthy and bloodless lives that sunbeams hate!

Heap these above the clay
Of beauteous Yesterday,
Ere uncompassionate earth enfolds his head;
While on through days to be,
With prescient eyes we see
Monotonous morrows their dull vista spread!

Wandering wide-sundered here,
But one faint hope shall cheer
The spirits that falter as they journey thus:
That where death dares not stray,
Re-arisen, our Yesterday
In patient immortality waits for us!

NATURE IN BONDAGE.

I SOMETIMES muse, in mournful way,
    Since tyranny should make us mourn,
Of how the city's cruel sway
    Chokes nature down with stony scorn;

Of how, where traffic's noises rave,
    Where dull roofs crowd and gray streets run,
The great primeval woods once gave
    Their leafy laughters to the sun;

Of how, in purlieus wrought for ease
    And all that luxury enshrines,
Perchance a briery dell heard bees
    Boom dreamy round its eglantines;

Of how in slothful haunts of wrong,
    Where vice and squalor darkly merge,
Perchance a crystal brook's pure song
    Has thrilled the violet on its verge.

And yet, intolerant of thrall
   Whose rigid rule she may not quell,
I mark, at many an interval,
   How fettered Nature would rebel.

For clear in squares of courtyard space,
   Or breaks of foliage rarely seen,
Or grass-rimmed pavements, I can trace
   Her timorous episodes of green.

But where some fragrant park sweeps wide,
   Her woful slavery gleams more plain,
As though its captive yearning cried,
   With lovelier eloquence of pain. . . .

Ah, Nature, find your comfort here,
   That still, for all man's power may do,
Your great heaven arches, year by year,
   Its chaste unvanquishable blue.

And still, though art with garish light
   Your duskier mood dismays and mars,
Pale o'er the city, night by night,
   Beam your undominated stars!

MYSTERIES.

WARM calms of heaven o'erbrood the earth;
    On scented sward my feet are pressed;
Spring breezes make melodious mirth,
    Yet silent awe pervades my breast;
To-day by Nature I am shown
Her marvellous elements alone.

I linger where the daisies throng,
    With golden disc on supple stem,
And careless of their beauty, long
    To unveil the impulse guiding them;
And wonderingly my soul receives
The resurrections of the leaves.

I cannot praise the emerald meads,
    Where pomp of lengthening clover peers,
Nor that green radiance of the reeds
    That cleave the marsh with slender spears.
My reverent heed alone I give
The miracle that has made them live.

Those blossoming trees whence odor floats,
    The full-fed rivulet's joy intense,
The ecstatic trills from feathered throats,
    Pierce me with strange bewilderments.
In all things lovely I would guess
The mystery of their loveliness.

But while I muse, the westering day
    Drops from the horizon's damask air;
The pastoral distances turn gray;
    New mystery deepens everywhere.
And high night brings, released from thrall,
The mightiest mystery of all.

SELF-DENIAL.

ABOUT her sweet majestic head
  The locks are simply filleted;
Serene she stands, with starry eyes,
Profoundly meek, sublimely wise!

A goddess of surpassing fame,
She sees no stately altars flame;
Within her grove there looms alone
A shrine of harsh Druidic stone.

But all the roads that hither wind
With splintry jeopardy are lined,
Where savage gales in shrouds of sleet
Like awful lovers wildly meet!

And through the years, to reach her home
A few pale silent pilgrims come;
On bleeding feet they bring to her
Their votive frankincense and myrrh!

And then the goddess in return,
Above her altar cold and stern,
Rewards their patient love, they say,
Through some divinely mystic way.

None know the guerdon she confers
Except these tireless worshippers,
Who rather would its joys command
Than hold the world in their right hand!

THE POET'S MASQUE.

TO-NIGHT the poet will give a masque,
  In his attic room, when the town is dumb,
And past a doubt it is surely true
That of all the multitude he will ask
Not any guest will refuse to come.
Grotesque in their contrasts, weird to view,
O'er the bare plank floor they will glide along,
The ghosts of story, the ghosts of song,
And the ghosts of history, two by two! ...
Napoleon the Great, in rough array,
With forelock dark on his brow serene,
With the snows of Russia, in some odd way,
On his massive coat well buttoned up,
Will bring the famous Egyptian queen,
Who hands him wine in a jewelled cup,
Where may be melted, for all we know,
Some marvellous pearl from tropic seas.
And after, closely following these,
Imperial Cæsar, with laurelled head,

And purple toga of stately flow,
A grave majestic measure will tread
(Paganini himself, it should be said,
Will fiddle till morning, fast or slow)
Beside sweet Marie Stuart, that star
And flower of beauty, whose tender style
Of making her deep eyes vaguely smile
Was the ruin of poor dead Chastelard!
And next, with crescent of gems half-hid
In his turban of splendid stuffs, behold
The illustrious Haroun Alraschid,
In silks of luxurious tinges clad;
And at his side, with tresses of gold,
And robes that no gorgeous words can paint,
Languorous, gentle and somewhat sad,
The bloom on her pure cheek rich though faint,
Comes floating, with loveliness untold,
Lucretia Borgia, that well-known saint.
And next grim Richard, third of his name,
Who swam through blood for the English crown,
With bad lean face, in its chronic frown,
And humpbacked shape, walking very lame,
Will bring the Spartan queen on his arm
In her classic dress with its glowing zone,
Greek Helen, fatally, grandly fair, —
In curve and coloring, eyes and hair,

So touched with a strange Olympian charm
Divinely and dazzlingly her own!
Then Faust, transformed to a gallant youth,
With velvet mantle and bending plume,
With curly blond beard and sword-hilt bright,
Will bring to the merry masque — why, whom
But **meek** Cinderella, in ragged plight,
Barefooted, and looking, poor young maid,
Very pretty but very much afraid!
And then, with solemn sculptural face,
That shows what his mournful heart broods o'er,
With head bowed low and loitering pace,
Pale Hamlet will come from Elsinore.
And tripping near him, in rompish grace,
Still rubbing both eyes from her long sleep,
With gypsy hat and a ribboned crook
And petticoat made of twenty hues
But worn not in any wise too deep
For showing her small rosetted shoes,
Up here to this lofty attic-nook
Will come, in search of her missing sheep,
Beside grave Hamlet, little Bo-Peep!
Then brave Godiva, clad in the light
Of her wondrous yellow hair, will appear
Beside Othello, as black as night,
With a great gold ear-ring in each **ear**

And a gaudy raiment of cachemire.
And next the beautiful Guinevere
Will come with that Spaniard, droll and grim,
The lank Don Quixote, leaning to hear
While she murmurs gracious words to him,
As though in her memory were not
Any Arthur or any Launcelot!

And so all night a crowd will stream
Through the poet's door, till rise of sun;
And though these masquers, every one,
Are the children of unsubstantial dream,
Yet the soul of a poet often sees
Traits far more real in things that seem
Than in life's most firm realities.
And not the haughtiest king may deem
His pride or pleasurement half so strong
When courtiers in his palace throng,
As the poet's, when through his attic door
Come gliding over the bare plank floor,
Grotesque in their contrasts, weird to view,
The ghosts of story, the ghosts of song,
And the ghosts of history, two by two!

A LEGEND OF HARVEST.

So long ago that history pays
   No heed nor record of how long,
Back in the lovely dreamy days,
   The days of story and of song,

Before the world had crowded grown,
   While wrong on earth was hard to find,
And half the lands had never known
   The forms and faces of mankind,

When just as now the years would keep
   Their terms of snows and suns and showers,
It chanced that Summer dropt asleep,
   One morning, in a field of flowers.

And while the warm weeks came and fled,
   In all their tender wealth of charm,
She slept, with beauteous golden head
   Laid softly on her milky arm.

She did not hear the waving trees,
　　The warbling brook she did not hear,
Nor yet the velvet-coated bees
　　That boomed about her rosy ear.

In many a yellow breezy mass,
　　The rich wheat ripened far away,
And glittering on the fragrant grass,
　　Her silver sickle idly lay.

But then at last, one noontide hour,
　　A bright moth, fluttering through the air,
Mistook her sweet mouth for a flower,
　　And waked her as he lighted there.

She rose in anxious wonder now,
　　To gaze upon the heightened wheat,
And saw its plenteous tassels bow
　　Dead ripe below the sultry heat.

Half crazed, she wandered east and west,
　　About the peaceful spacious clime,
Until at last, with panting breast,
　　She stood before old Father Time.

A LEGEND OF HARVEST.

With tears of shame she told him all,
    While pointing to the wheat unmown,
And said, "What power shall make it fall
    Ere Autumn's bitter winds have blown?"

Then Father Time, with laughter gay,
    Leaned low his frame and crooked his knees,
And tossed his white beard like the spray
    That crowns the crests of wintry seas.

"Oh, daughter, cheer your heart," he cried;
    "The wheat shall fall ere falls the night;
We two shall mow it, side by side,
    And reap it in the stars' pale light."

So Summer cleared her brow of gloom,
    And forth with Father Time she went,
And haggard age by youth in bloom,
    Above the tawny wheat they bent.

Ere fall of night the harvest fell;
    But since that season, fair and blithe,
As ancient annals love to tell,
    Old Father Time has borne a scythe.

A WHITE CAMELLIA.

IMPERIAL bloom, whose every curve we see
   So glacial a symmetry control,
Looking, in your pale odorless apathy,
   Like the one earthly flower that has no soul,

With all sweet radiance bathed in chill eclipse,
   Pure shape of colorless majesty, you seem
The rose that silence first laid on her lips,
   Far back among the shadowy days of dream!

By such inviolate calmness you are girt,
   I doubt, while wondering at the spell it weaves,
If even decay's dark hand shall dare to hurt
   The marble immobility of your leaves!

For never sunbeam yet had power to melt
   This virginal coldness, absolute as though
Diana's awful chastity still dwelt
   Regenerate amid your blossoming snow.

And while my silent reverie deeply notes
    What arctic torpor in your bosom lies,
A wandering thought across my spirit floats
    Like a new bird along familiar skies.

White ghost, in centuries past, has dread mischance
    Thus ruined your vivid warmth, your fragrant breath,
While making you, by merciless ordinance,
    The first of living flowers that gazed on death?

ROCKS.

THE whitening orchard scarcely stirs,
    While through it roam and sing
Those mild melodious pillagers,
    The breezes of late Spring.

In meadowy reaches, far and wide,
    No balmier May was born;
The expectant world is like a bride
    Upon her wedding morn!

All nature speaks its joy profuse,
    To see chill hours retreat,
Save, in their lethargy obtuse,
    These grim rocks at my feet.

Here timid mosses film their gray;
    Here starts the unfolding fern;
But still they bide, from day to day,
    Impenetrably stern.

Thus girt with life's exuberant grace,
  Yet thus from life exempt,
In their stolidity I trace
  The inertness of contempt.

With scorn they seem to brood, while these
  Ephemeral changes pass, —
The inconstant birds, the transient trees,
  The perishable grass.

"Light waifs," perchance their souls avow,
  "What kinship can you claim
With us that stood as we stand now
  Ere Egypt had a name?"

THE OLD GARDEN.

BEYOND the quiet homestead's lawn,
    In drowsy peace it lies,
Well from the passing gaze withdrawn,
    Its matted hedges rise.
Through solemn firs that veil the light,
    To reach its gate we press,
Ere softly breaks upon our sight
    Its halcyon loveliness.

Deep-rimmed with box, the paths we take
    Through realms of plenty range,
Where summer's mellowing fervors wake
    Perpetual charms of change,
And tender sounds, not told in words,
    Forever haunt the breeze,
A sense of epicurean birds
    And bacchanalian bees.

For bloom and fruit, in blended way,
  Here lightly gleam by turns;
Beside the currant's crimson spray
  The tiger-lily burns;
Or roses raise their balmy lips
  Near purple plums; or yet
The gooseberry's rounded amber slips
  Among the mignonette.

We see the ancient arbor loom,
  That bounteous vines enwrap,
And hear, within its fragrant gloom,
  Pale-glancing foliage flap;
Or when the wind of autumn grieves
  Round pomps her power shall strew,
We watch the grapes from tarnished leaves
  Hang dusty and dark-blue.

Shrewd wasps, in yonder jungle, haunt
  The blackberry's beaded gloss;
High stalks of maize in vigor flaunt
  Green flags and silken floss;
And here broad apple-boughs once more
  Hesperian wealth unfold,
Whose dragon is the worm at core
  That revels in their gold.

Now emerald melons wax immense,
    Or now with grandeur glows
The pumpkin's yellow corpulence,
    In smooth rotund repose.
Here, too, all homelier life occurs
    That household aims can please,
From curves of pimpled cucumbers
    To bowers of tangled peas.

So, thronged by growths of many a grade,
    The calm old garden lies,
Half mantled with monastic shade,
    Half bared to altering skies;
While sleepy spells are round it cast,
    That gently brood and muse . . .
Dead songs and sunbeams of the past,
    And immemorial dews!

A GERMAN CRADLE-SONG.

SLEEP on, my baby, sleep in peace, while day to dusk is turning,
And o'er the sunset's rosy calm one great white star is burning.
Their glooms against pale deeps of sky bold castle-walls are showing,
And through the shadowy valleyland the lovely Rhine is flowing.

Oh, all the sweet babes in the bourg for soft repose are weary;
The sunshine only brings them joy, but night is grim and eerie;
And, oh, I know that all night long, where reeds and sedges quiver,
The deadly Lorelei combs her hair beside the starlit river.

'Tis well through day for babes to play where sunbeams fling their lustre
Amid the arbor's yellowing leaves, and light the purple
 cluster.
But, oh, I know, when suns are low and stealthy darkness follows,
With fiery eyes and streaming locks the mad gnome
 haunts the hollows.

Oh, fair the river winds by day past towers and moss-
 grown churches,
Past hamlets whence the fisher sails to draw the net he
 searches;
But there like phantoms float all night, while shrill the
 owl rejoices,
Enchantresses in plumes of swans, that sing with angels'
 voices.

Sleep, baby, sleep; while mother-love your rest is
 warmly screening,
Above your cradle, meek and pure, our Lady's brows
 are leaning.
And, oh, I know that by her will some beauteous dream
 has found you,
Some dream from heaven that stoops and wraps its
 winsome wings around you!

CRICKET-CRIES.

IF the autumn winds are all
   In a tender sort of swoon,
You can hear the cricket call,
   Any autumn afternoon;
   And should you heed him, soon
You will hear, it may befall,
   Dreamy language wing its way
   Through his low and dreamy lay:

"By the mist-empurpled skies,
   By the red leaves lying sere,
I know that Summer dies
   In the lands that held her dear.
   And with his sparkling spear,
With his icy-brilliant eyes,
   Snowy-bearded Winter speeds
   On his whitest of white steeds!

"Oh, the days will shortly be,
   When here I must not cheep,
But in some black chink and wee
   Of some old fireside creep,
   To sleep and wake and sleep,
By the great log's yellow glee,
   And slowly find, no doubt,
   All the family-secrets out.

"From the hearth-fire's viewless flail
   I can see the spark-chaff fly,
Ere that ashy film and pale
   Furs the embers, by and by.
   How much better taste have I
Than my relative the snail,
   Toasting here, as fate appoints,
   My extravagant hip-joints!

"Hear the clock's quick tick, above
   Even the bitter north-wind's roar;
Hear the old grandam, like a dove,
   Coo her surreptitious snore;
   Hear the lovers laugh -- and more
See the lovers making love!
   And hear the purr of that
   Tawny sybarite, our cat!

CRICKET-CRIES.

" How I hearken, while I bask,
    To the hum the kettle wakes!
In his dull prosaic task
    How much merriment he takes!
    Ah, for me that kettle makes
All the nightingale I ask,
    Except it be, mayhap,
    The pine-log's bubbling sap!

" Why does Mabel grow so pink
    If she has not had a kiss?
It is fine, you lovers think,
    To be making love like this;
    Yet a pleasant blaze, I wis,
And a cosey little chink,
    Bring quite as much content
    To the cricket temperament!

" While the goldenrods, in seas,
    Plume the lanes and dales with gold,
While a glory smites the trees
    And the sumach-leaves burn bold,
    In my longing heart I hold
These, and pictures sweet as these,
    Waiting days more bleak and drear,
    That my fireside voice can cheer!

"Oh for winds of solemn tune!
   Oh for chilly-lighted skies!
Since she cannot die too soon,
   Oh, too slow the summer dies!" . . .
   Now in just this dreamy wise,
On an autumn afternoon,
   If your faith be good and strong,
   You can hear the cricket's song!

WOUNDS.

THE night-wind sweeps its viewless lyre,
    And o'er dim lands, at pastoral rest,
A single star's white heart of fire
    Is throbbing in the amber west.

I track a rivulet, while I roam,
    By banks that copious leafage cools,
And watch it roughening into foam,
    Or deepening into glassy pools.

And where the shy stream gains a glade
    That willowy thickets overwhelm,
I find a cottage in the shade
    Of one high patriarchal elm.

Unseen, I mark, well bowered from reach,
    A group the sloping lawn displays,
And more by gestures than by speech
    I learn their converse while I gaze.

In curious band, youth, maid, and dame,
    About his chair they throng to greet
A gaunt old man of crippled frame,
    Whose crutch leans idle at his feet.

Girt with meek twilight's calm and dew,
    They hear this battered veteran say
How once the black guns roared and slew
    On red Antietam's ghastly day!

He tells of hurts that will not heal;
    Of aches that nerve and sinew fret,
Where sting of shot and bite of steel
    Have left their dull mementos yet!

And touched by pathos, filled with praise,
    His gathered hearers closer press,
To pay alike in glance or phrase
    Response of pitying tenderness.

But I, who note their kindly will,
    Look onward, past the box-edged walk,
Where stands a woman, grave and still,
    Oblivious of their fleeting talk.

WOUNDS.

Her listless arms droop either side;
    In pensive grace her brow is bent;
Her slender form leaves half descried
    A sweet fatigued abandonment.

And while she lures my musing eye,
    The mournful reverie of her air
Speaks to my thought, I know not why,
    In the stern dialect of despair.

Lone wistful moods it seems to show
    Of anguish borne through laggard years,
With outward calm, with secret flow
    Of unalleviating tears.

It breathes of duty's daily strife
    When jaded effort loathes to strive;
Of patience lingering firm when life
    Is tired of being yet alive.

Enthralled by this fair piteous face,
    While heaven is purpling overhead,
No more I heed the old soldier trace
    How sword has cut or bullet sped. . . .

I dream of sorrow's noiseless fight,
   Where no blades ring, no cannon roll,
And where the shadowy blows that smite
   Give bloodless wounds that scar the soul!

Of fate unmoved by desperate prayers
   From those its plunderous wrath lays low;
Of bivouacs where the spirit stares
   At smouldering passion's faded glow!

And last, of that sad armistice made
   On the dark field whence hope has fled,
Ere yet, like some poor ghost unlaid,
   Pale Memory glides to count her dead!

REMEMBERED LOVE.

STILL as of old I seem to sit
   Where gods convene, with brows that shine;
The aroma still is exquisite;
   Still glows the unearthly wine!

Yet Hebe, urging me to sup
   With dimpled smile, no more I see . . .
But serving every golden cup,
   Glides dark Mnemosyne!

THE PUNISHMENT.

TWO haggard shades, in robes of mist,
    For longer years than each could tell,
Joined by a stern gyve, wrist with wrist,
    Have roamed the courts of hell.

Their blank eyes know each other not;
    Their cold hearts hate this union drear . . .
Yet one poor ghost was Launcelot,
    And one was Guinevere.

THE OLD BEAU.

HOW cracked and poor his laughter rings!
   How dulled his eye, once flashing warm!
But still a courtly pathos clings
   About his bent and withered form.

To-night, where mirth with music dwells,
   His wrinkled cheek, his locks of snow
Gleam near the grandsons of the belles
   He smiled on forty years ago!

We watch him here, and half believe
   Our gaze may witness, while he prates,
Death, like a footman, touch his sleeve
   And tell him that the carriage waits.

CONSOLATION.

WHEN all my life was wounded and forlorn,
    It felt the sacred influence wrought by thee,
As when sweet airy couriers of the morn
    Fling rosy prophecies o'er shadowed sea!

And now, though manlier force yet droop and fail,
    Though deathless memories haunt me past control,
Dear spirit of peace, thou art the nightingale
    That warbles amid the darkness of my soul!

ENVY.

WHERE spacious oak-trees thrive in rustling state,
    No fragile saplings quiver with weak hate.

Where palaces loom proud in sculptured height,
No lowlier roofs desire the earthquake's might.

Where groups of chaste-urned lilies whitely blow,
Dark soilure does not crave their balmy snow.

Yet what life ever towered, sublimely sweet,
But sneers, like adders, hissed about its feet?

MEISSONIER.

WATCHING your precious work, we vainly guess
    What miracle creates as potent fact
Such height in brevity, width in narrowness,
    And liberal vigor wed with cunning tact.

Your virile patience that no toil can crush,
    The more we muse upon we prize the more,
O Liliput Angelo, whose wizard brush
    Could paint a battle upon a *louis d'or!*

SONNETS.

BETROTHAL.

MY life, till these rich hours of precious gage,
    Was like that drowsy palace, vine-o'ergrown,
  Where down long shadowy corridors lay strown
The slumbering shapes of seneschal or page,
Where griffon-crested oriels, dim with age,
    Viewed briery terraces and lawns unmown,
    And where from solemn towers of massive stone
Drooped the dull silks of mouldering bannerage.

But now the enchanted halls break sleep's control,
    With murmurous change, at fate's predestined stroke,
    And while my fluttering pulses throb or fail,
I feel, in some deep silence of my soul,
    New strange delight awakening, as awoke
    The princess in the immortal fairy-tale!

CROWNS.

IT chanced that in the dubious dusk of sleep
    I seemed to attain that realm where mortals throw
   All gross mortality earthward ere they go
Forth as frail spirits amid death's hollow deep.
All folly and sin was here that life may reap,
    All desperate fear and hope, all joy or woe;
   And here all precious crowns the exalted know,
Lay gathered in superb tumultuous heap!

Stooping toward these, I marked with silent awe
    Their ponderous gold, or gems that beamed like day,
      Or lovelier laurel that grand brows had worn;
But hid below the beauty of each, I saw
    Continually, in grim recurrent way,
      The poignance of one small red-rusted thorn!

SATIETY.

AS when among dense-clustering vines we sit,
    Low-hidden from breezes round us, birds above,
  Even so they bowered themselves with fervid love,
And scorned life's busy murmurs infinite.
Then silently, as though by stealth should flit
    The expanded wings of some departing dove,
  Did gradual time to either spirit prove
That passion had eternally flown from it.

Shocked by the ruin of their radiant dream,
    With shuddering hearts that vaguely can divine
      To what strange bourne their fated feet are drawn,
They stare in dumb fear each at each, and seem
    Like two pale revellers on whose fruits and wine
      Flares the white merciless irony of dawn.

THE HOURS.

Once amid sleep I saw the twelve sweet Hours
   Go lightly along, gay sisters, hand in hand,
Some with gold flexuous hair and faces bland,
Some dusky as night and wearing stars like flowers.
"Ah, lovely!" I murmured,— but the secret powers
   Of slumber, issuing an occult command,
   Changed these fair wanderers to a mournful band
That moved with earthward brows through leafless bowers.

Then faintly across my dream a voice was borne . . .
   "The forms you first beheld, so blithe of mien,
   Look thus to eyes that hope's warm glory cheers;
While they that walk funereal and forlorn,
   Though still the same, by differing eyes are seen
   Through shadow of anguish and cold mist of tears."

INTERREGNUM.

WHEN fevered piteously with deep unrest,
   My heart through days of yearning drearier feels
Than though in lands whence faded summer steals
It shivered among sere boughs, an empty nest,
Then, following her capricious mood's behest,
   She at whose haughty feet my sad life kneels,
   With rosy sorcery for one day reveals
The illusive smile that is her loveliest!

Ah, then with happier change, I know not how,
   This nest, my heart, whose vacant silence grieves,
     Young carolling bird-throats charm, in sweet control;
But soon the inconstant smile grows dim . . . and now
   It is once more with me as though dead leaves
     Were falling amid the autumn of my soul!

THE DIAMOND.

TO shape my luminous life great ages went;
    For slowly its vivid fire had noiseless birth
Amid blank darkness of the old solemn earth,
Where long I abode in rayless discontent.
Then came at last discovery's dear event,
    That showed the world my rarity and rich worth,
    And made the light of my strange peerless mirth
Leap out to the loving sun, magnificent.

But now my cruel fate afflicts me sore;
    I, daughter of starshine, moonbeams, rain and dew,
      I, that in kingliest keeping should endure,
I, that majestic centuries labored o'er,
    Am tossed one evening by an amorous Jew
      In the lap of his luxurious paramour!

AMOUR TERRESTRE.

WHEN, grieving that your loveless heart relents
   By no compassionate sign, however shown,
  I lull to quietude despair's chill tone
With tender dreams of Heavenly recompense,
Hope brings me, at these hours, no joy intense
   That you, in habitations yet unknown,
   Hereafter may at last become mine own,
To adore among divine encompassments!

For should we meet where such far splendor lies,
   I could not reverence in rapture warm
     You dowered with chaste wings or the aureole's wreath;
But I should yearn to tear, like dark disguise,
   The shining immortality from your form,
     And find its earthlier womanhood beneath!

INDIAN SUMMER.

DULLED to a drowsy fire, one hardly sees
    The sun in heaven, where this broad smoky round
  Lies ever brooding at the horizon's bound;
And through the gaunt knolls, on monotonous leas,
Or through the damp wood's troops of naked trees,
  Rustling the brittle ruin along their ground,
  Like sighs from souls of perished hours, resound
The melancholy melodies of the breeze!

So ghostly and strange a look the blurred world wears,
Viewed from this flowerless garden's dreary squares,
  That now, while these weird vaporous days exist,
It would not seem a marvel if where we walk,
We met, dim-glimmering on its thorny stalk,
  Some pale intangible rose with leaves of mist!

BEES.

TRADITION'S favoring verdict would express
   In you all duteous thrift and toil extreme,
  Against gray wintry dearth, while summers beam,
Hoarding with zeal your honeyed bounteousness.
And yet in drowsy reverie I confess
   That booming now where flowery vistas gleam,
  Among these jubilant garden-paths you seem
The murmurous incarnations of idlesse!

Nay, more, you are like those pages, clad of old
By pampering lords in velvet and in gold,
  Who bore sweet amorous words, with cautious airs,
To delicate ladies in rich robes aglow,
Strolling down glades of shadowy Fontainebleau,
  Or loitering at Versailles on marble stairs!

A TIGER-LILY.

STRANGE that in your dark-dappled sanguine flower
   The sculpturesque repose can still endure
  Of that celestial lily, wrought so pure
It lives as chastity's white type this hour!
By what mysterious art, what baleful power,
   Did you, Diana of all blooms, allure
  From Nature's mood this Mænad vestiture,
And mock with gaudy tints your taintless dower?

Nay, long ago, I dream, through some warm dell
   Of Asian lands a wearied tiger stole
    Where you, in pale bud, felt your first dews cling;
And while he slept beneath you, it befell
   That all his deadly beauty pierced your soul
    And made you this fantastic sultry thing!

SLEEP'S THRESHOLD.

WHAT footstep but has wandered free and far
    Amid that Castle of Sleep whose walls were planned
By no terrestrial craft, no human hand,
With towers that point to no recorded star?
Here sorrows, memories and remorses are,
    Roaming the long dim rooms or galleries grand;
    Here the lost friends our spirits yet demand
Gleam through mysterious doorways left ajar.

But of the uncounted throngs that ever win
    The halls where slumber's dusky witcheries rule,
    Who, after wakening, may reveal aright
By what phantasmal means he entered in? —
    What porch of cloud, what vapory vestibule,
    What stairway quarried from the mines of night?

THE SPHINX OF ICE.

WITH dark, with frost, with silence for her shrine,
    Girt by her ghastly realms of dearth, despair,
  She reigns in solitude, contented there,
A goddess beautiful and saturnine.
Round her vast huddling bergs of frozen brine
    Jut spectral from the bitter North's gray air;
    Above her, weird auroras leap and flare,
And like swords' points the acute stars ever shine.

And venturous mariners, through weary years,
    Push up their bold barks, eager to discern
      Her great pale shape, her secret to entice,
Till wrecked, numb, doomed, with half insensate ears
    They hear long terrible laughter pealing stern
      In arctic mockery from the Sphinx of Ice!

ON THE NEWPORT CLIFFS.

AT either hand, as far as eye can trace,
    Lined with palatial dwellings, loom these heights,
  Having old ocean's glory of tints and lights
To murmur mellow rhythms against their base;
Or yet from many a porch of stately grace
    Clear down to where the extreme cliff's verge affrights,
  Having, through golden days and balmy nights,
Lawn after lawn to outroll its velvet space!

Ah, cruelty of luxury! . . . Dark for me,
    Remembering, musing, all your splendor frowns,
      Even here below this brilliant dome of sky!
For pierced with untold pity, I can but see
    Wan mothers, pent in rooms of torrid towns,
      Lean over gasping babes and watch them die!

NEWPORT, July, 1882.

TO MAURICE THOMPSON,

ON READING HIS "SONGS OF FAIR WEATHER."

LYRIST of woods and waters, loving best
   Pure Nature's alterant charms, thou art to me
A new Theocritus, whose gaze can see
New joys in that wide Sicily of thy West!
Yet now no longer thou companionest
   Meek flocks on dewy lawns, but wieldest free
   The bow of dead Diana, fallen to thee
By some divine and beautiful bequest!

Thy words, that often are leafage to the sense,
   Have strength like bark and grain of sturdy boughs,
   And rhythm as of a wind that sweeps and veers,
Till by the sorcery of their influence
   We steal down fragrant glooms where shy fawns browse,
   Or crouch where slim birds float from reedy meres!

TO OSCAR WILDE,

ON RECEIVING FROM HIM A BOOK OF HIS POEMS.

YOUR volume like a Provence lute antique
    Wed with a classic lyre were fitlier wrought,
  So richly opposite its theme and thought,
Its art so Gothic and its aim so Greek.
Till now we had deemed that one alone might seek
    From poetry what you with victory sought, —
  To blend those pure strains the Sicilian taught
With Spenser's line, luxurious and unique.

Nay, since your reverenced master dwells afar,
    It has been given your spirit, I am sure,
      To pass, deep-tranced by slumber's opiate sweets,
High up some white stair sheer to some white star,
    And meet in its immortal vestiture
      The splendor that men mean when they name Keats!

www.ingramcontent.com/pod-product-compliance
Lightning Source LLC
Chambersburg PA
CBHW020256170426
43202CB00008B/394